INTERVENTION IN
OCCUPATIONAL STRESS

INTERVENTION IN OCCUPATIONAL STRESS

A Handbook of Counselling for
Stress at Work

Randall R. Ross
and
Elizabeth M. Altmaier

SAGE Publications
London • Thousand Oaks • New Delhi

First published 1994, Reprinted 1997, 1998

Sage Publications Ltd
6 Bonhill Street
London EC2A 4PU

Sage Publications Inc
2455 Teller Road
Thousand Oaks, California 91320

Sage Publications India Pvt Ltd
32, M-Block Market
Greater Kailash – I
New Delhi 110 048

British Library Cataloguing in Publication Data

A catalogue record for this book is available from the British Library

   ISBN 0–8039–8672–6
   ISBN 0–8039–8673–4 (pbk)

Library of Congress catalog card number 94–065025

Typeset by Mayhew Typesetting, Rhayader, Powys
Printed in Great Britain by Biddles Ltd, Guildford, Surrey

Contents

1
Theories of Stress

This chapter is intended to introduce you, the reader, to theories of stress. Even though the topic of this book is occupational stress, the ways in which we understand, prevent and remediate occupational stress are heavily influenced by work that has been done in the area of general stress. Therefore, this chapter provides the foundation on which the rest of the book builds.

Stress is perhaps the most common problem of everyday life. The term 'stress' is so ubiquitous that it is used as a noun when we talk about being under 'stress', as a verb when events are 'stressing' us and as an adjective when modern life has become 'stressful'. Indeed, stress has come to characterize modern life. This chapter will begin by reviewing historical developments in the study of stress. Then, the chapter will consider three models of stress which differ in the perspective they take: first, stress as the response of the individual; secondly, stress as the accumulation of difficulties in an individual's environment; and thirdly, stress as the interaction of characteristics of the person and factors in the environment.

A related question that should occupy us in considering stress, and one that is of great interest to practitioners, is how people cope with stress. Stress is, after all, an ongoing process that can be worsened by our inability to control either the problem that is causing the stress or our reactions to the problem. Thus, this chapter will also describe the processes of coping and adjustment.

Historical Perspectives

Although stress is a concept that has interested psychologists for many years, early studies of stress were done within the field of medicine. In the first decade of this century, for example, physicians described the relationship between certain personality patterns and subsequent diseases. Even earlier, however, was the work of Claude Bernard in the 1860s who proposed that an individual's internal system should ideally remain constant in spite of external changes, a concept that was developed into the notion of **homeostasis** by Walter Cannon (1935). We will see later in this chapter that this concept of homeostasis has relevance for stress when we think about ourselves as a system that balances specific resources with the demands imposed upon us.

The link between external factors and the body's internal responses was furthered by Wolf and Wolff's (1943) study of changes in stomach activity that accompanied various emotions. For a particular patient, they could see that physiological changes, such as altered blood flow and changes in gastric secretions, were associated with changes in emotions. Much of their research was later developed into modern medicine's scientific study of psychosomatic diseases such as ulcers or asthma. Most of us have also experienced this link between external factors and bodily responses as when we have 'butterflies' in our stomachs before an important event or we feel flushed or lightheaded when we are anxious.

Stress as a concept has been studied for almost 100 years. This history of research and theory has given us several different ways to think about stress, since the research that has been reported has considered the experience of stress from several different perspectives. Three of these perspectives will now be described.

Stress as an Internal Response

The work of Hans Selye (1956) is generally considered the first major discussion of stress as a phenomenon in and of itself. Selye was interested in the response of the body to demands made upon it, and believed that this response was 'non-specific'. By this term, Selye meant that whatever the external or internal demand on the body, the person's response to stress followed a universal pattern. He termed this pattern the **General Adaptation Syndrome** (GAS).

The three stages of the GAS are illustrated in Figure 1.1. First is the stage of **alarm**. The alarm stage is the body's initial response to the stressor: there is a brief period of lowered resistance followed by a time of heightened resistance. In this stage, the body prepares itself for quick response by such means as increased heart rate and blood pressure and a release of glucose to provide energy for action. If you were crossing the road, and noticed a car speeding towards you, your rapid increase in speed from a walk to a run to escape being run over is an example of responding to stress in the alarm stage.

If the stressor is prolonged, the second stage is **resistance**. In this stage, the immediate responses of the alarm stage are replaced with responses that promote long-term adaptation. The concept of homeostasis described earlier comes into play during this stage, since the body must return to equilibrium. However, there is

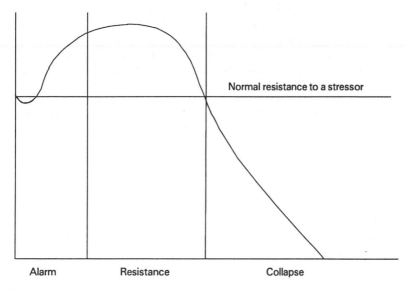

Figure 1.1 *General adaptation syndrome*

continuing effort on the part of the individual to adapt or habituate to the stressor during this stage. For example, after working in a noisy factory job for several months, Peter reports not being bothered by the noise. However, he does have frequent headaches and he has started grinding his teeth at night, resulting in occasional neck muscle spasms. In this case, the workers have learned to tolerate, over an extended time, the stress of excessive levels of noise in the job environment. (However, his physical symptoms suggest that the noise is still experienced as a stressor.)

The third stage is that of **collapse**. By this term, Selye meant that the body cannot go on coping with stress indefinitely. The energy for continued adjustment becomes depleted, and the individual becomes exhausted. Thus, the third stage is characterized by a loss of resistance to the stressor, and exhaustion, collapse and even death can occur. Prolonged stress during combat, when a soldier eventually collapses not from a wound but from accumulated fatigue, hunger, thirst, anxiety and tension, would be an example of the stage of collapse.

This model of stress has been challenged by researchers on two grounds. First, Selye's argument that every response to stress by every individual follows this pattern is difficult to accept. Research has indicated that the body's response to stress can vary, depending on the stressor. Secondly, this model proposes the same response for each stressor, whether external or internal in nature. However, we know that some stressors, particularly those that are complex and involve both internal and external demands, may create different responses from other stressors.

Thinking about occupational stress, this model can certainly account for stressors caused by certain job conditions, such as excessive noise. However, this model may be inadequate to explain our reactions to complex job conditions caused by many factors both internal to workers and external in the job environment, such as role ambiguity. The contribution of Selye's model should be acknowledged, however, since it advanced the study of stress as well as defined stress as an experience that can progress through different stages. It should also be noted that Selye believed in the concept of **eustress**, that is, stress that can be a motivation for growth and development, a positive stimulus for change. This stress has sometimes been called 'good stress'.

Stressors in the Environment

Another way to think about stress is as engineers do. In engineering, stress is defined as the total number of factors that strain a piece of equipment. Thus, equipment breaks down when the stress accumulates past a key breaking point. This concept has been applied to the study of stress in humans beginning with the work of Adolf Meyer in the 1930s. Meyer suggested that physicians use charts to record medical information such as dates of major illnesses, and environment situations, such as the death of a loved one or a change in job. His goal in these charts was to identify events that might have served to cause the individual to be susceptible to diseases.

This concept was further developed by Holmes and Rahe (1967). They defined **stressful life events** as those events which either signal or initiate significant life change in the individual experiencing them. The Social Readjustment Rating Scale contains 43 such life events, each of which is matched to a number of life change units. Some of these life events are clearly 'stressful', such as divorce (73 points) and the death of a close family member (63 points). However, other life events also are included, such as pregnancy (40 points) and vacation (13 points). The reason such apparently positive events are included is that they, as well as apparently negative events, cause the individual to have to make changes in life patterns. It is the accumulation of these changes that *causes* stress.

Holmes and Rahe were particularly interested in the relationship of these life events to illness. For example, they found that if life events involved 200 to 300 points, 50 per cent of the people accumulating these points within a year become ill. If more than 300 points were accumulated in a year, negative health effects were noticed in 79 per cent of the people (Holmes and Masuda, 1974).

This model has also been criticized. First, it is difficult to accept that part of the model that posits that everyone experiencing a particular life event experiences the same amount of life change and, therefore, the same amount of stress. In addition, it does not seem likely that different populations of people can each be accurately measured by a single life events measure. Further, there are some life events that are peculiar to certain stages of life, from adolescence to adulthood to elderly. However, this model is valuable in recognizing that we do experience stress from a variety of events, some quite routine. Also, the notion of stress as response to life *change* rather than to negative events alone is a provocative one.

Stress as an Interaction

The above two models emphasize either processes internal to an individual or events outside the individual. The third model of stress, and the model that is perhaps the most widely regarded today, is the **transactional model** (or interactional model) of Richard Lazarus (Lazarus and Launier, 1978; Lazarus and Folkman, 1984). This model defines stress as occurring when there is an **imbalance** between demands and resources, and emphasizes the ongoing nature of the balance or imbalance. In addition, this model says that environments can influence people and that people can influence environments; thus, any particular person–environment encounter has implications for both the person and the environment.

Lazarus' model begins when the person evaluates a particular event, situation, or demand. This evaluation, termed **primary appraisal**, is concerned with whether negative outcomes can occur in the encounter. An appraisal of harm means that damage has already occurred, while an appraisal of threat refers to harm that will likely happen in the future. Lazarus also defines an appraisal of challenge, where the individual believes he or she can achieve a positive outcome rather than only protecting against a negative one.

Secondary appraisal follows primary appraisal, and is the individual's attempt to define what coping options are available for

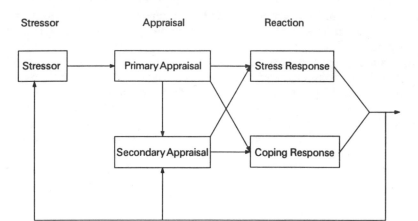

Figure 1.2   *Interactional model of stress and coping*

dealing with the harm, threat, or challenge. These options might be internal or external, and might be resources or responses. For example, a material resource in coping with the threat of a job loss is a loan of money from a relative. A coping response, in the same situation, might be to search for another job.

The model is an interactional or transactional one, in that the available coping resources have a strong influence on the future appraisal of the event or situation as stressful (see Figure 1.2). For example, John lost his job, but has immediate prospects for obtaining another job in a different company and he has family members who can loan him money while he is unemployed; his available coping resources would suggest that John would evaluate the situation as less threatening than would Steven who also lost his job but has no immediate prospects for a different job and no available financial resources from his own savings or from family upon which to depend. Consider, too, Gloria who has been thinking about making a job change; the loss of her job might be the 'push' Gloria needs to make this change. Thus, while the job loss would be threatening, it is also challenging and might be experienced by Gloria as exciting as well as anxiety arousing.

The difficulty, and the attractiveness, of this model is its flexibility. The model allows us to understand stress as the combination of personal issues and concerns, which change over time, as well as the resources and responses that a person can call upon in times of stress, which also change over time. These responses, in turn, affect the initial situation or stressor, and may cause us to appraise it, or think about it, differently. Thus, the stress response is truly a transactional one, where the balance of demands and resources defines stress: if the demands are greater than the resources, then stress occurs. The reverse is also indicated: if resources are available to meet the demand, then the secondary appraisal might be one of challenge rather than harm or threat, and thus would be less stressful to the individual.

Chapter 8, which contains material suitable for presenting at a workshop or group, has several handouts pertinent to stress. Handout 1 provides a series of definitions of stress, including the possible health consequences of stress. Handout 2 presents items in the stressful events inventory, so that a person can calculate his or her stress points. Handouts 3, 4, and 5 assist individuals in identifying symptoms or signals of stress and distress. Handouts 6 and 7 allow an assessment of stress vulnerability.

As an example, consider Pamela who is attending a stress identifer workshop conducted by a facilitator using the above-mentioned materials. Pamela's life stress points totalled 250, due mostly to a serious illness and recent divorce. Since Pamela lives alone, she has lapsed into very negative health habits which are revealed on the inventory contained in handout 6. She smokes over two packets of cigarettes each day, drinks about six cups of coffee, eats irregularly, exercises rarely, and stays up late each night drinking beer and watching television. This 'picture' of stress would also be reflected by handouts 4 and 5.

Coping as an Internal Response

Whatever model of stress is adopted for use in thinking about a particular situation, it is clear that what the person does in coping with a stressor is important in understanding the stressful situation as a whole. Many theorists have considered characteristics of people who seem to cope effectively with a range of difficult situations in an effort to identify personality traits linked with successful coping. One such trait is a **sense of coherence**, proposed by Antonovsky (1987) as a way of seeing the world that emphasizes it as predictable and comprehensible.

There are three themes in the sense of coherence: comprehensibility, manageability and meaningfulness. People high on comprehensibility believe their life and the experiences in it are ordered, structured and predictable as opposed to random and confusing. The theme of manageability means that people believe they have resources at their disposal that are adequate to meet the demands placed upon them. Last, meaningfulness speaks to the way in which people believe life and their experiences make sense to them, and also that many of life's problems and challenges are worth their investment of time and energy.

It is important to note that Antonovsky believes this sense of coherence exists within various aspects of life. Thus, for example, a sense of coherence would apply to relationships within the family as well as to employment. It is particularly interesting to apply this concept to job-related transitions such as retirement. A worker facing retirement must move from valuing and being valued in work situations to developing new ways in which to receive this positive feedback. The concept would suggest that a person with a strong sense of coherence would accomplish this transition more effectively than a person with a weak sense of coherence.

Coping as Environment Resources

Coping with stressors and difficulties can be eased by having resources available in the environment. One such resource is the availability of **social support** (Cobb, 1976). It is clear that having supportive friends and family plays a large role in determining how well people adapt and adjust. In fact, the role that social support plays in assisting individuals to deal with stressors has been termed the **buffering effect**: namely, that stressors will have negative effects on people who have little social support, but less negative effects on individuals with stronger systems of support in their environment (Cohen and Wills, 1985). Social support, therefore, 'buffers' the individual against the potential negative effects of stressors.

How does social support exert these positive influences? Researchers have developed several ideas of the ways in which supportive others can help us cope with stress. The first is perhaps the most obvious, and was alluded to earlier with the example of a family member providing a loan to a person threatened with losing a job: social support that provides tangible assistance (namely money, tools, food, a place to live, etc.) will help individuals deal with stress more effectively than individuals without this assistance.

Social support, however, can be provided in less obvious and more 'psychological' ways. One of these is that social support can influence the process by which a person decides that a situation is stressful. In the model of stress developed by Lazarus, for example, there are two ways in which appraisal occurs: one in which the stressor is appraised as harmful, threatening or challenging and a second in which resources are appraised as available or not available. If one's supportive group can assist an individual in deciding that a situation is not threatening but challenging, for example, then less stress will result. Similarly, if an individual believes that support is available from a group of friends or family, then perceived coping resources are increased.

Last, social support can reduce stress by the effect such support has on our feelings. If social support helps us to feel loved and accepted by persons important to us, then threats to esteem posed by the stressor will not be as harmful. This model of esteem support provided by others is particularly important in some job stressors, especially job stressors that threaten esteem such as retirement or job termination. Chapter 3 will consider social support in more detail.

Coping as an Interaction

It is clear that coping is a complex combination of things that people can do to deal with stress. Lazarus' model, in particular, emphasizes this aspect of coping since it says that coping consists of all of the cognitive and behavioural efforts that a person makes to manage the demands of a stressor. These efforts can be focused on the problem, such as what might occur when we seek information about what needs to be done to change our own behaviour or the problem in our environment. However, these efforts can also be focused on our own feelings about the problem, as we would cope by trying to regulate the emotional distress caused by the situation.

This coping process is termed **transactional**, in Lazarus' theory, since he believes that our coping efforts, whether directed towards a problem or towards ourselves, in turn affect our ongoing appraisal of the stressor. For example, if John is having an argument with his boss at work about increased responsibilities, John might initially believe he can cope by changing the boss's mind (primary appraisal as challenging, coping as problem-focused). However, if he tries to change his boss's mind about the situation, and fails to do so, that failure will be 'fed back' into the system (primary appraisal) and John may come to believe that no other problem-focused strategies will work (secondary appraisal) (see Figure 1.2). Thus, the balance between demand and resource has shifted, and we would expect increased stress and accompanying emotional distress for John.

Conclusions about Stress and Coping

The models of stress and coping described in this chapter give us many valuable tools for understanding the nature of occupational stress and in intervening to reduce the manifestations of stress. They also lead us to ask several questions which will reappear in this book. How do individual differences (such as sense of coherence) affect coping at work? Do similar work stressors cause similar levels of occupational stress for different types of workers? How do occupational stress models lead to counselling interventions and to methods for evaluating the effectiveness of these interventions? Chapter 2 will discuss occupational stress more directly, and will begin to answer some of these questions.

2
Understanding Occupational Stress

Steve, a 29-year-old chemical engineer, was in the seventh month of a start-up project. His role required him to work 12 to 14 hour days and usually one weekend day as well. While the project was coming along well, he was experiencing symptoms of 'occupational stress'. He was highly stimulated by the challenge and potential of the project, but was torn by the needs and wants of his young family. He felt he could not give his spouse and two children the time and energy he wanted to. No one was complaining loudly, but 'seven months is a long time, with a possible five more'. He began asking himself questions: Can I keep up the pace? How do I balance career and family needs? What are my needs? Where do I draw the line? If I limit my work time, will there be negative career repercussions?

The problem of occupational stress is being increasingly recognized. As the case of Steve suggests, the many dimensions of the problem challenge us to understand, prevent and reduce stress related to the workplace. In this chapter, we will define occupational stress and describe how occupational stress is manifested in the workplace. If you refer to the diagram outlining stress in Chapter 1 (Figure 1.2), this chapter will describe the 'reaction' part of that diagram. Chapters 3 and 4 will then introduce factors influencing occupational stress that 'cause' the effects we will be discussing in this chapter.

What is Occupational Stress?

Occupational stress can be defined in ways that match the ideas presented in Chapter 1. That is, occupational stress can be considered as an accumulation of stressors, job-related situations that are considered 'stressful' by most of us. For example, a stressful work situation might be one with many demands placed upon the employee, with little time for meeting them, and with increasing criticism from supervisors. Alternatively, we could think about job stress as the stress experienced by a particular individual on a particular job. Such a consideration might include whether the employee was experienced or new to the job, whether he or she routinely coped well with circumstances or was a poor coper, and what type of personality he or she brought to the job.

Both of these definitions would be good ones because they isolate certain aspects of the job environment or the person at work. However, as we noted in Chapter 1, these two types of definition ignore the interplay between the person and the environment. Therefore, in this chapter we will define **occupational stress** as the interaction of work conditions with characteristics of the worker such that the demands of work exceed the ability of the worker to cope with them. This definition fits the person–environment context that we outlined in Chapter 1 and allows us to examine the joint contributions to occupational stress of worker characteristics, job conditions and their interactions.

What are the **symptoms** of occupational stress? Beehr and Newman (1978) outlined three categories of symptoms that occur under conditions of occupational stress: psychological symptoms, physical health symptoms and behavioural symptoms. We will examine each of these types of symptoms separately.

Psychological symptoms are those emotional and cognitive problems that occur under conditions of job stress. Job dissatisfaction is the most likely consequence of occupational stress, where a worker is dissatisfied with his or her job, dislikes coming to work and finds little reason for doing well on the job. Additional psychological symptoms are depression, anxiety, boredom, frustration, isolation and resentment. Some of these symptoms are problems in themselves in that they can make job stress worse: for example, a worker who finds himself increasingly frustrated by job conditions may become depressed and withdrawn, and therefore is less able to cope with job problems in ways that would improve his work conditions and enhance his mental outlook.

Physical symptoms are more difficult to define because, while particular work conditions have been linked to certain physical ailments and conditions, it is difficult to know how much these ailments are 'caused' by the job itself versus other aspects of the worker's life. For example, if a worker is suffering from headaches on a regular basis, and blames work for the stresses that cause the headaches, that attribution of the causes of the headaches is certainly as likely as blaming family troubles, but not necessarily completely true. However, there is research evidence that consistently links occupational stress with certain physical symptoms and diseases.

One of the most common physical health symptoms of job stress is cardio-vascular disease. There is significant research that links stressful work conditions to the risk factors of cardio-vascular disease; the interested reader is referred to a review by Sutherland and Cooper (1990) for more information on this research. There is also an established link between job stress and gastro-intestinal conditions, such as ulcers. Other physical conditions that may result from ongoing occupational stress are allergies and skin diseases, sleep disturbances, headaches and respiratory diseases.

Behavioural symptoms occur in two categories. The first are symptoms that can be said to 'belong' to the worker. This group includes such behaviours as avoidance of work, increased alcohol and drug use, overeating or undereating, aggression towards fellow workers or family members, and interpersonal problems in general. Other behavioural symptoms 'belong' to the organization: absenteeism, leaving the job, accident proneness and loss of productivity.

In summary, occupational stress can be visible to an observer with symptoms that describe an individual, such as ulcers or a depressed mood or increased hostility. However, occupational stress can also be defined by individual performance in a work environment, such as increased absenteeism or loss of productivity. An example of the latter is Kathy, a historically dependable and valued employee, who had begun a pattern of 'short call-ins' (calling in to report on absence immediately before the start of the work day), lateness and several instances of absence without an excuse. Efforts by supervision to address this situation were not as successful as desired. Kathy was referred to EAP (see Exhibit 2.1) because of signs of high stress, the source of which was unclear because Kathy's stated reasons for her behaviour did not fit and because her behaviour did not change.

Through EAP assessment – a confidential process – Kathy related she was dealing with a physically and emotionally abusive spouse who was also drinking excessive amounts of alcohol. Referring to herself as a 'private person' she chose not to confide in anyone at work. Conceding that her work was affected, by trying to solve the situation on her own, she thought she would not jeopardize employment.

How does Burnout Relate to Occupational Stress?

The term **burnout** is a popular one, and many people confuse burnout with occupational stress. However, as noted by Pines and Aronson (1981), burnout occurs as a result of ongoing job stress. Thus, burnout is itself one of the most important consequences of uncorrected job stress.

Burnout has three parts. The first is that of physical exhaustion. Recall the model of stress developed by Hans Selye (1956) that we presented in Chapter 1. In this model, Selye argued that stress which occurs over a period of time depletes the reserves of the individual and a state of exhaustion ensues. This physical exhaustion is one of the components of burnout. Individuals who are burned out report intense weariness, often combined with an inability to sleep. In addition, symptoms of low energy, chronic fatigue and weakness are common.

The second part of burnout is emotional exhaustion. In a manner parallel to how physical resources become depleted under extended conditions of occupational stress, emotional resources can also become depleted. The burned out worker manifests feelings of depression, helplessness and hopelessness. Satisfactions that had previously been available to the worker through leisure, family and friends, and work diminish and overall life satisfaction is reduced.

The third part of burnout is mental exhaustion. Negative attitudes form towards work, towards the clients served by the company, and towards fellow workers. There is a dehumanizing aspect to these attitudes, where burned out workers fail to respond to the feelings of others. These negative attitudes and dehumanizing tendencies can 'spill over' to family and friends.

The consequences of burnout, noted by Pines and Aronson, are severe. Workers who are burned out may leave not only their jobs, but also their professions. This loss is particularly severe in the human service professions, such as teaching and counselling. The cost to society of losing these well-trained and highly experienced professionals is a high one. Other workers may leave their jobs, but stay in the same organization or within their profession. Still other workers use job advancement, perhaps to administrative levels, as a way out of their current job situations. While this option can be an effective solution for some persons, the result may be negative for the company or organization if the new supervisor brings the negative attitudes and responses to the new position and to his or her new supervisees that characterized his or her work before the promotion.

Other workers who are burned out remain in their jobs, gradually losing any enthusiasm for it and for their own personal and professional development. Such workers present particular challenges for intervention, since they may grow unwilling to accept a different job that might be more interesting or involving even when offered. These are the workers that are 'counting the years' or even months to retirement and providing an organization with personnel 'dead wood'.

Costs of Occupational Stress

Our discussion of stress and occupational stress would suggest that the costs of occupational stress are high but also difficult to determine accurately. Both of these conclusions are correct. It is impossible to arrive at an accurate determination of costs associated with occupational stress because of the complexity of the problem. However, we are able to determine certain relevant facts. If occupational stress is thought of in terms of the individual's response to job conditions, then statistics on the prevalence and cost of emotional and behavioural responses are relevant. For example, alcoholism costs US industry approximately $20 billion each year. A mental illness such as depression, which can be a result of occupational stress, incurs costs in health care expenses and in lost worktime – it has been estimated that depression costs the US economy $30 million each year.

Other costs of occupational stress are those resulting from the job performance of the employee. Absenteeism, for example, is a particularly costly problem – estimates of the effect of absenteeism suggest that 4 per cent of work hours are lost because of absent workers. This estimate translates into millions of dollars annually.

Perhaps the biggest cost of occupational stress, and the one most difficult to calculate, is the effect of errors made by workers who are working under impaired conditions. An air traffic controller making a single error can incur incalculable costs in human lives. Many accidents on the job can result from occupational stress – estimates suggests that in the US over 2 million workers a year suffer a disabling injury from a work accident, and 15,000 persons die each year from a work accident.

Other and more insidious costs are those to human lives. Relationships can be ruined, children can suffer the effects of parents' job stresses, job opportunities can be lost, and the quality of life can be affected. The cost in human quality of life, combined with the actual economic cost, reveal occupational stress to be a problem of staggering cost and critical importance. For this reason, many companies are combating occupational stress with Employee Assistance Programmes. The cases of Steve and Kathy, described earlier in this chapter, are cases brought to Dow Chemical Company's EAP (see Exhibit 2.1).

Exhibit 2.1

Occupational Stress and an EAP

Bill Pagel

The Michigan Division of the Dow Chemical Company in Midland employed 5,100 engineers, scientists, manufacturing operators, laboratory technicians, skilled craftsmen and support personnel in 1991. The site produced agricultural chemicals, plastics, consumer products, specialty and pharmaceutical products. Historically, Dow's policy of 'running lean' has resulted in few if any employees being laid off during tough economic times. At the same time, expectations of employee performance runs very high. Quality, teamwork and continuous improvement are a few of the concepts that have kept Dow a 'premier' company, and an exciting company to work for.

As in many companies, occupational stress within Dow is recognized to be a major factor to be dealt with. Dow also recognizes that non-work stressors have a significant impact on business outcome. Michigan Division's Employee Assistance Programme has existed for approximately 45 years. Initially, like most EAPs, the focus was on alcohol abuse in the workplace. In recent years, EAPs have addressed problems on a much wider scale, called the 'broad brush' approach. A client or customer walking into an EAP counsellor office may present a problem scenario that stems from either work or personal life, but usually a combination of both. The EAP counsellor must be prepared to assess both areas for possible stressors.

Steve, being pulled in two directions, both powerful and within reason, came into the EAP office not so much for guidance as for support in his struggle. Through 'ventilating' and 'thinking out loud' he came to satisfactory conclusions and decisions. He decided to discuss the situation with his supervisor, which resulted in his delegating some aspects of his job. Very often, a person in Steve's situation, because of feeling stressed, overassigns self-responsibility to counteract the feeling of not being in full control. This, of course, leads to more stress. Personal health habits, such as good diet, exercise and enough sleep are usually disregarded with lapses into a 'grabbing' mode becoming a coping style. Steve gave himself permission to take time for a more healthy lifestyle, an image of himself he had been in conflict with. With the delegation of pieces of his project, Steve spent more hours with his spouse and children. Family satisfaction increased. Several months later, his project was very successfully completed and Steve moved on to a new opportunity. He no longer questioned his values or the direction of his career.

When the major source of stress is from an employee's personal life, there is almost always an effect on work life, sometimes to the point of seriously affecting the employee's work performance. Much of EAP work is in family/marital issues. With the divorce rate as high as it is, businesses have to pay attention to the behaviour and needs employees exhibit during the break-up of a marriage, which often takes a year or more. The period of time prior to 'the filing' is typically chaotic, especially when there are children, and when only one spouse wants the divorce. In Michigan, the two to six months following the filing may cause disruption of desirable work performance. EAP counsellors are often called upon, either through self-referral or supervisory referral due to performance problems, to serve as a support, guide or treatment provider during this time. Supervisory referrals to EAP are not viewed as disciplinary, but are intended to help confront the causes of the performance problem.

In Kathy's case, EAP intervention included ruling out abusive behaviour towards the children, support and encouragement to Kathy with active referrals to appropriate community agencies that address abuse and alcoholism, and interaction with supervision as needed, with Kathy's permission. Once Kathy realized that the company's goal was to help her return to her usual highly regarded performance, not put her job in jeopardy, her stress level was reduced, which gave her additional energy to face her personal situation.

In the future, Employee Assistance Programmes' involvement in addressing stress in the workplace will include not only an individual case approach, but also a group perspective. The EAP in the Michigan Division has been requested to work with 'natural work groups' when most of the group appear to be experiencing stress. A family system approach helps define the nature of the stress and offers a method by which to provide direction.

Bill Pagel, M.S.W., is an EAP Counsellor for Dow Chemical Company, Michigan Division, Midland, Michigan.

3
Individual Variables that Influence Occupational Stress

This chapter and Chapter 4 will describe factors which influence the experience of occupational stress. As has been discussed in previous chapters, there are several routes through which occupational stress can be said to be 'caused': factors tied to the individual, factors tied to the workplace, and the interaction of these factors. In this chapter, we will review concepts that have been studied in relation to occupational stress which are specific to the individual and his or her unique experience in the workplace. Two general categories of concepts will be covered: personality characteristics and coping resources and responses. (It should be noted that characteristics of the individual's life outside of the workplace which affect his or her experience of job stress will also be included in this chapter, since such characteristics have increasingly been shown to influence occupational stress.) Chapter 4 will describe concepts tied to the workplace itself.

Personality Characteristics

It makes sense that an individual behaves at work, responds to the demands of his or her job, and interacts with co-workers in ways that mirror his or her interactions in other life domains. Therefore, it is of interest to us to understand how personality characteristics studied in other domains affect a worker's experience in a job situation. In this chapter, we will consider two personality characteristics (Type A Behaviour Pattern and sense of control) as well as the individual characteristic of gender.

Type A Behaviour Pattern
One of the ways in which we think about people and their personalities is a concept that has been very popular among professionals and the lay public alike, namely Type A Behaviour Pattern. In the 1950s, a team of medical scientists investigating the role of various risk factors in heart disease discovered that certain cases of heart attack could not be explained by conventional medical reasons, such as family history of heart disease or history

of high blood pressure. These researchers came to focus on emotions and personality as the link to heart disease, and developed a concept they termed **Type A Behaviour Pattern** (Friedman and Ulmer, 1984).

Type A Behaviour Pattern, or Type A personality, is characterized by several components. The first is a sense of time urgency. Since Type A's are 'driven' to achieve more and more, the accomplishments must fit into less and less time. Thus, Type A's often do more than one thing at a time, are impatient while 'wasting time' by mundane activities such as waiting in line or sitting in the car, and speak at a rapid pace. The second component is aggressive striving: a drive to achieve that ignores the feelings of others and is highly competitive. This drive to achieve is manifest in all of life's activities, not just ones in which competition is usually a part. Type A individuals may be competitive in their work environment, in their family lives and even in their leisure time; consider Frank, a Type A person who cannot enjoy a game of golf unless he is beating his companions. The third component is a high level of hostility. Type A people may be resentful and suspicious of others, and may be easily angered by people in their environment. For example, Pamela is described by others at her job as cynical, aggressive and hostile in her interactions with people.

Recent research has suggested that Type A behaviour is not as strongly related to coronary heart disease as first thought. However, hostility has been shown to have a strong relationship to heart disease (see Smith and Pope, 1990). Although we do not know why this link exists, there may be two reasons. First, hostile individuals may be more physiologically reactive than non-hostile individuals. Recall the model of stress presented in Chapter 1, where ongoing stress can result in a stage of collapse. It may be that hostile individuals, being more physiologically reactive, reach the collapse stage more quickly than non-Type A persons. Secondly, hostile individuals may stay aroused for a longer period of time; they do not 'cool down' as quickly as non-hostile persons.

It is important to know that both hostility, and Type A Behaviour Pattern, can be changed. Friedman and his associates (Friedman *et al.*, 1986) have shown that people who received regular counselling regarding behaviour change had a marked decrease in Type A symptoms and had less chance of a second heart attack. Roskies (1987) provides a complete review of research on counselling interventions for Type A Behaviour Pattern for the interested reader. In general, these interventions have helped Type A persons focus their values, relax more effectively, manage their anxiety and build more leisure time into their activities. Several of the handouts in Chapter 8 present materials to use in teaching relaxation skills (see especially handouts 19 and 20).

How does Type A Behaviour Pattern fit into our discussions of work stress? Type A persons are more likely to experience occupational stress simply by how they view the world. As an example, consider Edward. He resents any other person's work-related achievements and he is not liked and supported by his co-workers. He is more likely to be bothered by the normal stresses at work, and less likely to be able to adjust his behaviour to normal stresses. Because of the ways in which he approaches his job, such as his intense drive to succeed and his impatience with interruptions and interference, he is more likely to experience occupational stress and less likely to deal with it effectively.

Sense of Control
When used by psychologists, 'control' refers to the perception by an individual that his or her actions result in particular outcomes, particularly as those outcomes are important for that person. Control may also refer to an individual's perception of free choice from among alternatives. Control has been shown to have important effects on people's response to stress, and its role in occupational stress is equally important.

It is critical to note that the above definition emphasized the person's *perception* of control as opposed to actual control. In fact, researchers have shown that people often overestimate the degree to which they have control over certain outcomes. Studies that investigated people's perception of control over certain outcomes that were clearly due to chance alone, such as coin tossing, revealed that people believe they have control over some outcomes for which no actual control is possible. It is interesting to speculate on why people's belief in their own control persists in the face of evidence to the contrary. It is possible that such beliefs motivate people to continue to work hard in the face of difficult circumstances. However, research with victims of tragic events (see Bulman and Wortman, 1977) suggests that it may be more helpful to a victim to believe that an accident is *not* under one's control, a belief that lessens the possibility of self-blame for a bad outcome. Thus, the helpfulness of believing in control may depend on the particular situation within which control is studied.

Actually, exercising control by making decisions about work is an important aspect of reducing or avoiding occupational stress. Research conducted by Frankenhaeuser and her colleagues (see Frankenhaeuser and Johansson, 1986 for a review) revealed that workers who were able to self-pace their work, that is, work at their own pace and decide on their own tasks, had fewer symptoms of stress than workers who did not have this control over their work environment. Many of the aspects of stressful job environments to be discussed in the next chapter, such as pacing, emphasize the importance of the employee knowing that he or she has control over key aspects of the work environment and over the actual tasks that are completed during the work day.

Psychologists have also been interested in the effects of the *absence* of control, particularly repeated demonstrations that we cannot control certain outcomes. Seligman (1975) postulated the existence of a concept he termed 'learned helplessness': namely, that in situations where our actions repeatedly fail to affect outcomes, we come to expect that our responses will not affect outcomes and we stop trying. In his initial research, Seligman used a situation where dogs could not escape electric shock. When the dogs were later placed in a situation where escape was possible, the dogs did not attempt to escape. Seligman hypothesized that the initial learning of response–outcome independence conditioned the dogs to remain passive and not attempt to escape. Hiroto (1974) demonstrated a similar phenomenon among humans using inescapable noise. People who were exposed to inescapable noise did not attempt to escape later noise when escape was possible. In addition, these 'helpless' subjects were poorer at problem solving than were subjects who were only exposed to escapable noise.

Abramson *et al.* (1978) considered the above research in the light of what people think about and say to themselves about the failure to have control. In particular, they hypothesized that, when confronted with an instance of response–outcome independence, people can attribute their lack of control to several different causes. If this lack of control is attributed to causes that are internal to the person, such as lack of ability, then the helplessness will be more costly in loss of self-esteem and initiative. However, if the lack of control is attributed to external causes, such as other people or the task itself, then less damage ensues.

Consider this research applied to a situation at work, where Kathy is confronted by an angry boss for the second time in a single day. If she says to herself, 'The boss is angry with me again. I can never do things right, and I will probably be sacked from this job soon', then Seligman and colleagues would suggest that Kathy will become depressed and lose initiative at work because the attribution was to an internal cause – ability – that is not likely to change in the future. However, if Kathy makes an external attribution, such as 'The boss is really having a bad day. I will stay with this task and finish it as quickly as possible and then get out of his way', then less debilitating results will occur because her attribution is to an external cause that is not likely to recur (the boss's bad day).

How does control, either actual or perceived, fit into our discussion of occupational stress? First, understanding occupational stress involves knowing the degree to which an employee feels he or she has control over important aspects of work, both the tasks that are involved and the work environment. As will be discussed in a later chapter, increasing the employee's control over key aspects of work can reduce occupational stress and enhance performance. Secondly, research on learned helplessness suggests that workers who are 'burned out' may have come to believe that they have no control over important outcomes when such control, in fact, exists. It might be helpful to correct these perceptions about lack of control.

In summary, control is a critical component of occupational stress. Workers who experience low control combined with a highly demanding job are particularly prone to occupational stress. Further, the lack of control that characterizes the lives of most workers in their jobs is the biggest contributor to occupational stress. Two aspects of control are important: the control experienced by workers (perceived control) and the control that is exercised by workers over their jobs. This point will be returned to in Chapter 4.

Gender
Although gender is not a personality characteristic, a person's gender is part of what the individual brings to the workplace, and thus will be considered in this chapter. There has been an increasing interest in the effects of gender on the experience of workers, particularly given the growing number of women in the workplace and in jobs that have traditionally been regarded as the province of men. This changing role of women in society and in the workforce has led to greater consideration of the influence of gender on occupational stress.

Smith (1979) pointed to a 'subtle revolution', where the pattern of women's lives has changed from one where family responsibilities and work roles were sequential, not simultaneous, to one where family and work responsibilities are occurring at the same time. Statistics support this contention. In 1988, for example, 56 per cent of all American women were members of the paid labour force, a statistic expected to rise to 62 per cent by the year 2000. Perhaps more startling is the fact that there are significant changes in the employment of mothers with young children. Sixty per cent of all mothers are employed by the time their youngest child is four years old, and nearly half of all mothers of children less than a year old work outside the home (Hayghe, 1986). Thus, women are experiencing the stresses of multiple roles, particularly in the context of no previous experience to serve as a resource for managing these multiple roles.

Sorensen and Verbrugge (1987) suggested three models of thinking about how participation in the workforce results in health outcomes, models which are instructive in considering the potential effect of the greater work participation of women. First is the **health benefits** model, which puts an emphasis on the benefits of employment. For example, employment can lead to greater financial resources, enhanced self-esteem and greater opportunities for social contacts, all likely to lead to enhanced health. This model would suggest that the participation by women in the labour force would maintain and even enhance women's health, potentially by increasing their resources for dealing with stress.

Alternatively, employment by women could serve to increase their **job stress**, the second model. Although working can provide employees with many rewards, it can also serve as a source of significant stress. Dangerous job conditions, repetitive work which can lead to physical damage, and job stress itself pose potential for significant harm to women workers.

The third model is the **role expansion** model, which suggests that the greater opportunities for role involvement inherent in work can lead to increased satisfaction and enhanced self-esteem. This model also suggests that work can be a source of reward that can protect the individual from loss in another role.

Research suggests that women experience certain stressors to a greater degree, and with different effects, than do men. For example, Wortman *et al.* (1991) considered the role overload of women professionals with pre-school children. In this research, they interviewed women over a period of time concerning role conflict and role strain. One of their primary interests was in the conflict these women experienced between their work and family responsibilities. The frequency of these conflicts was striking, since the women reported such conflicts virtually daily, and the average frequency was two to three times a week. Their husbands, however, reported work–home conflicts on an average of once each week. Interestingly, the husbands' estimates of the frequency of their wives' conflicts were significantly less than the actual frequency.

Wortman *et al.* also considered women's work in the context of

spillover. This term represents the influence of one domain on another, such as might occur when Don carries home his resentment of an argument with a boss and is bothered all evening by that. Spillover can occur from work to home, such as late evening work preventing Cheryl from attending a family gathering, or from home to work, as when Mike must miss work to care for a sick child. It has been hypothesized that, because of their greater involvement in family responsibilities, women are particularly prone to experiencing negative effects from spillover. Wortman *et al.*'s data supported this contention, revealing that the women's job overload was associated with increased marital strain and dissatisfaction; the husbands also reported that the quality of their marriage was suffering because of the job demands of their wives.

As noted by Frankenhaeuser *et al.* (1991), we do not know much about women's health nor do we understand the implications for women's health of their increased involvement in the labour force. In addition, research has often treated women as a homogeneous group, 'averaging' across the effects of different types of occupations and jobs as well as across the different life stages of women. It is important that research be done which does not treat all working women as alike. Another concern is that many of the occupational stressors peculiar to women, such as conflict with home responsibilities and the experience of harassment on the job, are chronic in nature. Yet, much of the research on occupational stress in general has considered it as isolated incidents. Clearly, the research to be conducted during the 1990s must move to a more complex understanding of the effects on women and their greater participation in paid employment.

Exhibit 3.1 describes the experience of a worker with spillover, and discusses how she coped with her work stress.

Exhibit 3.1

Work and Family Stress

Becky Durham

Family stress has impacted my career/jobs in many ways. The first of these was my marriage. Being part of a dual career relationship provides ample opportunities for stressful situations that influence jobs. Early in my career, I took temporary positions in which I did not have to make long-term commitments to allow for flexibility until my husband had completed his degree. A layoff and then termination of my spouse's positions brought stress into our lives. As a result of these transitions, we moved several times to new cities and I too had to leave my positions and find new employment. I elected to take several jobs, to gain experience in my career field, that involved extensive travel or living away from my spouse. This option involved a sacrifice of our time together to benefit establishing our careers.

A second family factor that has caused stress on the job was the addition of children to our family. With both of our careers under way and ten years of marriage, we thought we were ready and prepared for children. However, nothing can prepare you for the impact children have on your life. After having a child, I have now needed to worry about child-care arrangements. During the first year, we had over five different day-care providers. The stress this caused on my performance at work, and my inability to concentrate, was incredible. Illness is another major issue faced when raising children. Having a sick child at home and pressing priorities at work are enough to make anyone feel crazy and guilty. In fact, the whole process of child bearing is a large stressor. I have suffered two miscarriages and one stillbirth in trying to have children. These losses cannot be compartmentalized and remain 'at home'. The effects of losing these children were carried with me into my work environment as well.

Thirdly, the lives of extended family members have also contributed to stress in my life. I was significantly affected when my father needed treatment for alcoholism and then again during his two years of unemployment. The diagnosis of cancer for a very special grandmother and her death also impacted on my life tremendously, which in turn infiltrated into my job.

As a career counsellor at a private, religiously affiliated university, I have had the fortune of being in a supportive work environment. During my five years with this institution, co-workers have provided the type of culture that encourages family values and that realizes life roles are intertwined and cannot be separated from my daily work. The support has come in various forms from administration, supervisors and colleagues. I have the opportunity to have a flexible work schedule and set my own hours, making it possible for me to work around the needs of my child-care arrangements. It also affords me the luxury of rearranging my schedule for appointments that must be scheduled. I have been provided paid leave of absences. This benefit allowed me to participate in family week during my father's alcohol treatment as well as have six weeks after the birth of my stillborn daughter. With the birth of my other daughter, I also received six weeks paid leave, and I built in some vacation time and unpaid time for a three month leave. In anticipation of my second child, I had negotiated with my supervisor and his boss for a four month leave with a part-time return. When my daughter is ill, I am allowed to use my sick leave time to stay at home with her. Co-workers have pulled together and provided assistance to cover my work at times when I was absent, and they provide morale boosters in the form of cards, flowers and calls.

My philosophy on stress is that it is an inevitable part of life, so I take care of myself in the hopes that the effect it has on me is as minimal as possible. I have found that nothing beats stress relief as well as routine exercise. I attempt to maintain cardio-vascular and weight training workouts five to six days a week. An additional way I have coped is to make a conscious decision to work in a job, career, department and institution that supports my values of family and life balance to maintain a healthy lifestyle. I do not believe the circumstances in my life are that unusual in relation to the influence of family stress and its impact on jobs. Through self-management and supportive work environments, the impact it has can be recognized and effectively handled.

Becky Durham is a Career Specialist at the University of St Thomas in St Paul, Minnesota.

Coping Resources and Responses

An alternative way to view factors tied to the individual which influence the experience of occupational stress is to consider the individual's coping resources and responses. Recall the interactive model of stress presented in Chapter 1, where the perception of available coping resources and responses affected the individual's appraisal of a situation as stressful or not, as well as influenced his or her coping response. In this section we will consider one major coping resource, social support, and we will discuss general coping styles and responses.

Social Support
In the early 1980s, the California Department of Mental Health distributed car bumper stickers that read 'Friends can be good medicine' as part of a state-wide public education effort promoting

the positive effects of supportive social relationships (Hersey *et al.*, 1984). This effort was undertaken because of the increasing recognition that social support has positive benefits for an individual's mental and physical health. The importance of social support in occupational stress is critical, since support from co-workers and from supervisors has been shown to be a strong influence on occupational stress. This section will review research on and models of social support and discuss its role in occupational stress.

There has been much interest in understanding social support and an accompanying need to define it. Social support can be understood quantitatively, as in the number of persons we have whom we would call our 'friends', or the number of people we have social contact with in a typical week. When we consider support in this way, we are concerned with an individual's 'network', the web of social relationships which surround an individual. These relationships are then studied in terms of measurable aspects of the network: its size, its geographic dispersion, its density (the degree to which members of the network are themselves acquainted with each other), and frequency of contact between the individual and the network members.

However, social support can also be studied qualitatively, that is, by understanding the individual's perception of the degree to which the supportive relationships he or she has meet his or her needs. In this case, an individual may have few friends but believe these friendships meet most of his or her needs. Many researchers have proposed definitions of social support (see Cohen and Wills, 1985) and these many definitions share several similarities. A principal similarity is that the definitions emphasize a prime role of social support as **emotional support**, when individuals feel they have other people to turn to for comfort during difficult times. An additional similarity is that these models emphasize **social integration**, when people feel they are part of a larger group where their interests and concerns are shared. Thirdly, support can operate as **tangible support**, where our requests for money, tools, assistance with a task and so on are positively met. The fourth similarity is that support can provide **informational support**, where we can depend on others for advice concerning a problem. The fifth similarity is **esteem support**, where social relationships serve to help people feel better about themselves and their skills and abilities.

Although not mentioned by all theorists, Weiss (1974) adds a sixth provision of social support, and that is the opportunity that social relationships gives us to **nurture others**. In fact, Weiss' model of social support encompasses all of these six components of social support, and research using this model is what we will emphasize in this section. Weiss' model is outlined in Table 3.1.

Table 3.1 *Weiss' (1974) Provisions of social support*

Assistance related	
Guidance	Providing information or advice
Reliable alliance	The assurance that others can be counted on during times of stress
Non-assistance related	
Reassurance of worth	Recognition of one's skills and abilities by others
Opportunity for nurturance	The sense that others rely on one for their well-being
Attachment	Emotional closeness from which one derives a sense of security
Social integration	A sense of belonging to a group with which one shares interests and concerns

What are the effects of social support on health? First, support has a direct positive effect for everyone. This notion emphasizes the positive effects of support provided by a large network of social relationships and the accompanying set of social roles in various life domains (such as work, community). This model would suggest that support is positively related to health since support provides everyone with a sense of well-being, some degree of predictability and stability in life, the ability to avoid negative outcomes or experiences, and the emotional support and encouragement of close and intimate friends.

An alternative model of understanding the beneficial efforts of support is the **buffering model**, or an interactional model. The buffering model (see Cohen and Wills, 1985, for a review) suggests that social support operates as a buffer for stress. Thus, when individuals are under low levels of stress, both those with high social support and those with low social support will show few negative effects. However, during stressful times, individuals with low levels of support will begin to show negative effects; individuals with high support will show few negative effects since their support 'buffers' them from the effects of stress. The experience of Becky in Exhibit 3.1 describes the buffering influences of her employer's and colleagues' support during stressful times.

How does support work, either in a direct or a buffering way, to reduce or prevent stress? Recall the interactional model of stress presented in Chapter 1. In this model, potentially stressful events lead to a primary appraisal and a secondary appraisal. During primary appraisal, having social support could prevent an individual from defining a situation as stressful because of his or her perception of available resources. For example, if Christine knows that others can provide necessary information, or equipment, or assurance during a stressful event, she does not see her situation as stressful. Alternatively, during secondary appraisal, support may assist Jim in determining an adequate solution to the problem at hand or may help his negative feelings about an uncontrollable situation, thus reducing the impact of stress in an ongoing way.

How might social support relate to the experience of occupational stress? It seems reasonable to believe that support would assist workers to deal with occupational stress in the same way that it does in regard to stressors in other life domains. Research indicates that this assumption is indeed correct. For example, a study of social support and teacher job stress conducted by Russell *et al.* (1987) revealed that teachers who had higher levels of support that gave them reassurance of their worth reported less emotional exhaustion at work and indicated a greater sense of personal accomplishment. Perhaps most significantly, this support was especially helpful when it came from supervisors.

A similar study of hospital nurses (Constable and Russell, 1986) supported this idea, in that reassurance of worth was related to occupational stress, with those nurses who received reassurance of their worth from their supervisors reporting the lowest amount of occupational stress. As will be described in the following chapter, interventions which focus on increasing social support in the work setting have been used with some success to combat occupational stress.

Coping Responses
As we noted in Chapter 1, 'coping' refers to those actions that a person takes in response to a stressor, whether real or perceived. Pearlin and Schooler (1978), for example, defined coping as 'any response to external life strains that serves to prevent, avoid, or control emotional distress' (p. 3). External events experienced by the person can stimulate the coping efforts as well as the person's 'inner environment', the thoughts and feelings the person is experiencing in relation to the event and the coping response.

Early attempts to define coping viewed it as a cluster of intrapsychic processes by which a person's psyche was protected from threat. This conceptualization was rooted in psychoanalytic theory and emphasized coping as ego defences. Thus, for example, the coping mechanism of denial protected the individual from external threat and thereby preserved mental health. Later and more recent conceptualizations defined coping in a more balanced way. That is, the purpose of coping is broader than protecting the individual from threat; rather, coping means those responses which deal with a problem, reduce psychological distress, or change the meaning of a situation.

We distinguish between coping resources and coping responses. The former are what is available to people to assist them in coping; social support represents a coping resource as do certain psychological characteristics, such as hardiness and a sense of coherence. The latter are the actual responses that people make in response to stress. In this section we will describe coping responses and their function as well as consider whether coping varies as a function of life domain, a topic with some importance for understanding occupational stress.

How might we classify coping responses? There are some classifications which attempt to summarize coping responses within one major theme. For example, Lazarus and Folkman (1984) divided coping into two categories based on the *focus* of coping: problem-focused coping are those responses that modify or eliminate the problem, while emotion-focused coping are those responses which manage the emotional consequences of the stressor.

Alternatively, we could consider the *purpose* of coping. Pearlin and Schooler (1978) have divided coping into three categories: responses that change the situation, responses that change the meaning of the situation so that a stressful consequence is less likely, and responses that control the stressful consequence after it has occurred.

Within the first category are responses that modify or change a stressful situation. It is interesting that Pearlin and Schooler's study of over 2,000 community living adults revealed that this category of coping responses is least likely. Three typical responses that change situations were identified: negotiation in marriage, discipline in parenting and direct action in occupational settings. The latter has implications for us in our consideration of occupational stress, since taking this route was associated with reduced stress for those persons who reported using it. Pearlin and Schooler speculated that this category of response is less frequent because people lack the ability or knowledge to change a situation, fear negative consequences if direct action is taken, or believe (perhaps correctly) that a situation is resistant to change.

A second category of responses are those that change the meaning of a situation. It could be said that these coping responses function cognitively to 'neutralize' the stressor, since the meaning of the situation that serves to determine the threat associated with it is changed. One such response is positive comparison, making one's own situation appear better by comparing it with that of others who are worse off. Another example of a coping response in this category is selective ignoring, changing the focus of attention from the troublesome aspect of the situation to one which is more rewarding. In work, for example, Bob might focus on the stimulation provided by his job if he is unhappy with the pay, or he might consider the opportunities provided for advancement by a job that he does not like.

The third category of responses are those that manage stress, that attempt to reduce the negative impact of a stressful situation. There are many such responses: denial, accepting hardship, avoiding the problem, ventilating feelings, and so on. As we noted in Chapter 1, the use of these responses 'feeds back' into the loop, so that the stressor may be perceived as less stressful if negative emotional responses are successfully managed.

What coping mechanisms work best under what circumstances is a critical question and one that research has yet to solve. Indeed, the problem is so complex that a single answer is probably not possible. However, there are questions for which data are available that are of interest: Are some coping responses and resources generally more effective than others? Is it better to be able to use many coping responses, or are there one or two that are so effective that they are best in every situation?

The data of Pearlin and Schooler (1978) revealed significant differences in effectiveness of coping responses among life domains. For occupational stresses, for example, an effective coping method was to devalue work, so as to keep it and its stressors in a secondary place, and gain some distance from it. Other effective methods were those associated with the types of personalities possessed by the respondents, such as being confident and having a sense of control over the situation. It should be noted, however, that Pearlin and Schooler's data also revealed that occupational stressors were more difficult to manage than stressors associated with other life domains, such as marriage and parenting.

It seems intuitively obvious that being able to cope in more than one way would assist one in dealing more effectively with life's stressors. In line with this suggestion Pearlin and Schooler (1978) found that having more possible coping responses was associated with more effective coping, although this relationship was weakest for occupational stressors.

Perhaps the most interesting question in studying coping is

whether what people *do* or who people *are* is more effective. The traditional view of personality would suggest that being a certain way would predispose a person to more effective coping. Alternatively, it could be said that certain domains call forth certain coping responses, and thus what we do is more of a determinant of our effectiveness. Pearlin and Schooler analysed their data by role area and determined that effectiveness was related to the life domain of the stressor. Within marriage, for example, coping responses (what a person does) were more important in determining stress than were resources (who a person is). However, within occupational stress, stress was more a function of resources than responses, resources defined as both environmental (that is, social support) and psychological (that is, sense of mastery, coherence).

What does this discussion of coping mean to our understanding of occupational stress? It suggests, first of all, that coping may and does vary across and between life domains, including which responses are most effective in reducing stress. It may be that occupational stress is one area in which actual control is more difficult to exert, and thus the best coping methods are those which emphasize dealing with situations rather than changing them. Practitioners working with employees who are stressed must remember that work stressors are different from stressors in other life domains and must help the employee think about these work stressors as separate from stressors in other contexts.

A second consideration is the variety of coping responses and resources that can be brought to bear on a problem. If Peter is coping with all work stressors with one coping method, no matter how successfully that method may have worked in the past, it is likely that the method will not continue to be successful. A practitioner should assist him to gain new coping responses and resources. The means by which this assistance can occur will be considered in Chapters 5 and 6.

How to measure coping responses, or use of resources, is an interesting question important to researchers as well as practitioners. The most common form of measuring coping is the 'Ways of Coping' scale, developed by Lazarus and Folkman (1984). This scale focuses on measuring the use of many different coping methods, although Lazarus and Folkman differentiate between coping which is problem-focused, those strategies that attempt to change a situation, and coping which is emotion-focused, those strategies which change how the person feels about the situation.

More recently Carver *et al.* (1989) have developed a measure of coping which presents the test taker with coping strategies grouped into 10 categories: active coping (making a plan and following it), suppressing competing activities, positive reinterpretation (trying to gain personal meaning from an experience), acceptance, seeking emotional social support, seeking instrumental support (getting advice), denial, focusing on emotions, behavioural disengagement (giving up) and mental disengagement (daydreaming about other matters). Table 3.2 contains a sample item for each of these categories.

Table 3.2 *Sample coping items*

Active coping: 'I concentrate my efforts on doing something about the problem.'
Suppressing competing activities: 'I put aside other activities in order to concentrate on the problem.'
Positive reinterpretation: 'I try to see the problem in a different light, to make it seem more positive.'
Acceptance: 'I accept that the problem has happened and that it can't be changed.'
Seeking emotional social support: 'I get sympathy and understanding from someone.'
Seeking instrumental social support: 'I ask people who have had similar experiences what they did.'
Denial: 'I refuse to believe the problem happened.'
Focusing on emotions: 'I get upset, and am really aware of it.'
Behavioural disengagement: 'I just give up trying to reach my goal.'
Mental disengagement: 'I daydream about things other than the problem.'

Weintraub *et al.* used this scale to study people's responses to a variety of stressful events which varied on their controllability, a dimension that has already been identified as one that is important to occupational stress. In their results, uncontrollable events (as compared with controllable ones) produced more denial, more focus on emotions, more disengagement, and less active coping. Interestingly, people who were generally optimistic used more active coping than people less optimistic and they were also more accepting of situations and found more meaning in them (fitting in with our earlier discussion of a sense of coherence).

Summary

The research discussed in this chapter has highlighted several important themes. First, people's personalities can make occupational stress worse, as might Type A Behaviour Pattern. However, certain personality traits, such as a sense of coherence, can help occupational stress by making difficult situations more manageable. Secondly, it is important to consider people's home lives when thinking about occupational stress, since stress at work can spill over to home and stress at home can spill over to work. Thirdly, work stress may pose special difficulties in coping because the lack of control over major work stressors makes typical coping responses ineffective. Thus, interventions for occupational stress which target either environmental sources of stress or personal responses to stress are critical.

4
Work Setting Variables that Influence Occupational Stress

In Chapter 3 we discussed those factors pertaining to an individual and his or her life both in and outside of work that are believed to affect occupational stress. In this chapter we turn to a discussion of factors in the workplace linked to occupational stress. It is important to note that an interaction between the individual and the work environment most completely describes stress. However, we have undertaken a separate discussion of these two sets of variables to aid in the development of more comprehensive interventions. In other words, effective intervention programmes might include a focus on changing or improving the individual's skills in coping with the stress along with changes in the work environment itself.

A number of different kinds of occupational stress factors in the work setting have been presented. In this chapter we will discuss specific work setting variables linked to occupational stress and how they relate to intervention. The system for describing work setting variables in occupational stress presented is based on category systems proposed by a number of researchers. More importantly, the category system presented here is designed to offer a guide in designing intervention programmes since the categories in this system represent key intervention points that a practitioner might consider within an organization or work setting. These categories are role characteristics, job characteristics, interpersonal relationships, organizational structure and climate, human resource management practices, and physical qualities and technology. The remainder of this chapter focuses on each of these areas.

Role Characteristics

Psychosocial factors in the workplace have been proposed as a way of understanding occupational stress. In particular, researchers have applied 'role theory' to understanding stress problems at work and to examining how role pressures contribute to occupational stress. Ivancevich and Matteson (1980) noted, for example, that role pressure occurs when an individual's expectations or demands conflict with expectations and demands of the organization. Role characteristics have been said to be the most widely investigated organizational condition in stress research (Schuler, 1984). At least four sets of role characteristics have been proposed: role ambiguity, role overload, role underload and role conflict.

Role Ambiguity

One work setting variable linked to occupational stress is termed **role ambiguity**. This role characteristic has been defined as a job situation in which there are inadequate or misleading pieces of information about how an individual is supposed to do the job (Beehr, 1985a). Additionally, role ambiguity is said to result when an individual's role is not clear, including lack of clarity about the objective of a job or the scope of an individual's responsibilities (Ivancevich and Matteson, 1980). Although role ambiguity is inevitable in most organizations, organizations need leaders to clarify this ambiguity in the roles that employees must fulfil. The real stress of role ambiguity is experienced when individuals are prevented from being productive and achieving. In addition, stress resulting from role ambiguity is experienced when an individual loses a sense of certainty and predictability in the work role (Schuler, 1984).

As an example of role ambiguity, consider a new employee in an organization. This employee will need to learn the responsibilities and tasks required for the new job along with the less clearly defined aspects of the organization, like organizational climate and unwritten organizational rules. Consider this conversation between a manager and a trainee who has been on the job for two months:

Manager: Well, Dave, you've been with us two months. How have things been going?
Trainee: I must admit that while I'm glad to be here, I *am* feeling overwhelmed.
Manager: I'm sorry to hear that, Dave. This is all news to me. What exactly is causing your problem?
Trainee: Well, it's just that this is so much to learn, I don't know how to keep up.
Manager: But Dave, we sent you to several training seminars and we haven't even given you any project assignments – you've only been asked to read the training manuals.
Trainee: I know you've been very generous with the time you've allowed for training and I'm really not having a problem with the technical part of the job. I think I'm more worried about the other part of the job. I'm trying to figure out how I am supposed to act, whom I'm supposed to meet and which things I should be doing to avoid overstepping my role as a rookie.

In this example, the manager might help Dave by discussing some of the informal organizational rules or by helping him identify important people that Dave might want to meet in his first year with the company. Leaders of organizations attempt to help new employees deal with role ambiguity by offering job training and orientation.

Role ambiguity is not, however, only the experience of new employees. Even veteran employees experience role ambiguity. For example, imagine Jan, a customer service representative, who is employed by a food brokerage company that undergoes major reorganization. As a part of this reorganization Jan's job changes from servicing accounts for all products (frozen foods, canned goods and dairy products) in one state to servicing only frozen food accounts at warehouses throughout the country. This change might leave Jan uncertain about how to do the new job even though she is familiar with the product and with the tasks involved in being a good customer service representative.

Role Overload

Another role characteristic which has been identified as a source of occupational stress is **role overload**, which occurs when an individual is not able to complete the work that is part of a particular job. Role overload might be compared with what happens to an electrical system in an engine. If there is too much electricity in the system it will become overloaded and the entire engine might malfunction. In terms of role overload in work, an individual in a work group might malfunction where there is too much work to be done.

The concept of 'too much work' can be divided into two categories. The first of these categories is labelled **quantitative** role overload, which is said to occur when the individual does not have enough time to complete all of the work that is required of a job (French and Caplan, 1973). Picture a secretary who is asked to move from providing clerical support for two full-time professional staff members to four full-time professionals. This secretary might experience quantitative role overload if the job change meant that all work could not be completed in the previously required 40 hour work week.

The other kind of role overload is **qualitative**. In this case, 'too much work' is not associated with time but instead involves not having adequate skills to do a particular job. Qualitative role overload occurs when employees do not believe they can perform adequately with the effort or skills they possess. As an example of qualitative role overload, imagine the employee who has worked for 10 years as a production engineer. If this employee is suddenly promoted to manage the entire production engineering department, she might not have the necessary skills to function as a manager. The work required as a production engineer might not have included such managerial tasks as hiring/firing employees, conducting performance appraisals, or managing the department budget. This same situation happens in many organizations, where people are continually promoted until they reach a job they cannot do. Peter and Hull (1969) termed this phenomena the 'Peter Principle' which describes the qualitative role overload that can result when a formerly successful employee is moved to a new job that requires skill he or she does not have.

Role Underload
Another role characteristic related to being stressed in a particular job occurs when a person's skills are underutilized. The resulting stress is called **role underload**. While role overload represents a demand, role underload is characterized by constraint. Role underload is said to be present when employees have too much ability for the jobs they hold.

As early as 1911, in his discussion of scientific management, Taylor (1911) noted the negative effects that can arise when an individual is overskilled for a job. Classic examples of role underload occur in production jobs at the bottom of the organizational hierarchy. In these jobs, workers might be required to do simple, repetitive tasks that could be completed by a machine. Other kinds of jobs, however, are not exempt from role underload. Imagine Tom who worked as a computer programmer for seven years at a large financial institution. Because of improved technology and increased computer expertise among employees in departments throughout the company, Tom was required to do less programming. In fact, Tom eventually was only needed to monitor the computer systems every 30 days when month-end reports were compiled. The role underload that Tom experienced was so severe that he eventually became dissatisfied and left the company.

Role Conflict
In addition to role ambiguity, **role conflict** has been studied as another factor that could affect perceived stress at work. Role conflict is said to exist whenever compliance with one set of role pressures make compliance with another set of role pressures objectional or impossible (Beehr, 1985a; Ivancevich and Matteson, 1980). At least four different types of role conflict have been identified.

Intersender role conflict is a situation in which expectations, pressures, or demands from one person conflict with the demands of another person. For example, a sales representative for a life insurance company might experience pressure from a boss to deal with each account quickly to increase the volume of accounts and sales. At the same time, this sales representative might feel a demand from individual customers to spend more time explaining possible life insurances plans and to allow customers ample time to make good decisions about insurance problems.

Intrasender role conflict occurs when the same member of the role set asks an employee to perform activities which are mutually exclusive or incompatible. Imagine a psychologist working at a university counselling centre. This psychologist could experience intrasender role conflict if the director of the counselling centre gave two incompatible messages. For instance, the director might say the psychologist needs to increase the number of outreach workshops that are offered to faculty, staff and students. At the same time, the director might say that all staff psychologists need to double the number of individual counselling sessions that are offered each week. Given the total number of hours in a work week, the psychologist could not possibly meet both requests.

Person-role conflict happens when the demands of an individual's work roles conflict with the individual's personal values. The classic example of person-role conflict would be the medical doctor who is asked to complete a medical procedure that he or she considers to be morally objectionable. Still another example might be found in the corporation accountant who is asked to falsify company records to ensure that certain taxes could be avoided.

Inter-role conflict is the final type of role conflict to be discussed here. Inter-role conflict results when an employee experiences conflict between the expectations and demands of people at work and the expectations and demands of people outside of work. For instance, being asked to work late into the evening on one's wedding anniversary could represent a situation that might lead to inter-role conflict. As another example, a social worker employed by a country agency might be asked by an administrator to report the names of county residents who are abusing welfare benefits. Inter-role conflict would occur for the social worker if the request of the administrator was in conflict with the mandate of the social work profession to provide confidentiality to clients who are involved in counselling.

In summary, the extensive application of role theory in under-standing occupational stress has been important in conceptualizing the psychosocial nature of work-related stress. The many different kinds of role stressors that have been described here should lead the practitioner to conclude that it is important to focus on the unique situation that faces each worker. Interventions that will aid in dealing with the problems faced by workers in stressful situations will be described in Chapters 6 and 7.

Job Characteristics

Another set of factors linked to occupational stress are characteristics of the job itself. This area of research has traditionally focused on jobs that are labelled 'blue collar'. In more recent years, however, study of job characteristics has been expanded to include other kinds of work. Much of the research about blue collar jobs has been found to be applicable across many different kinds of jobs and occupations, and a number of aspects of the work environment can contribute to occupational stress. In this section, factors are described that are specific to the way in which a job is performed or accomplished. Four different job characteristics are outlined below: work pace, repetition of work, shift work and task attributes.

Work Pace

One of the characteristics that influences occupational stress is the pace at which an individual must do work. Work pace is concerned with who or what controls the pace of work, particularly the amount of control an employee has over the work process. Salvendy (1981) presented two classifications of work pace. The first, **machine pacing**, represents a work condition in which the speed of operation and production are controlled by some source other than the employee. An easily recalled image of machine pacing would be a worker on an assembly line who must attach one part to an engine as it moves along the line. The other type of work pace classification, **human pacing**, refers to a situation in which the employee or some other human in the work setting controls the process of work. The employee might control the pace of work himself or herself, as in the case of self-pacing. Other examples of human pacing might involve other people in the work setting. In socially paced work, for instance, the other people in an individual's immediate work group might influence the pace of work. This form of paced work might be observed in the self-managed work teams that are found in organizations attempting to use total quality management (TQM) practices.

As an example of the stressful effects of increased pacing, consider this description from Julie who works as a clerk in an insurance company.

> Stress ... yes I have plenty of it on my job. With our company's emphasis on Total Quality Management (TQM), we have reorganized the way our teams are set up. It used to be that I processed claims for one agent and he was aware of how much work he was giving me. Now with the reorganization, I receive claims from three agents who cover a five state area. All three of the agents think their claims are most important and each one of them has slightly different ways of wanting forms done. Because these three agents have no contact with each other, they have no idea when I am overwhelmed with work from the other agents. I used to like my job but lately I've felt so stressed that I've considered looking for a position with a smaller firm.

At least three factors are consistently linked to stress-related difficulties resulting from pacing (Smith, 1985). The first of these factors is the potential lack of control the worker perceives he or she has over the work process. Short time cycles for tasks (for example, having only a few seconds to complete a task before moving to the next task) seem to be especially problematic. A second factor is the amount of repetition that characterizes the pace of work. (This factor will be discussed later in this section.) The final factor is the amount of pressure or demand the employee feels in relation to pacing work. Those workers who experience a work pace as full of pressure or highly demanding are likely to experience the greatest amount of work stress. A worker might experience high pressures from a boss to produce or perform more quickly. An employee might also feel a self-imposed demand to perform if work pace is tied to compensation (for example, being paid for the number of products produced in one day).

Repetition of Work

As noted in the discussion of work pace, the amount of repetition in work is another job characteristic that can influence occupational stress; the more repetitive a particular job, the more likely the job incumbent is to experience stress (Wallace *et al.*, 1988). The actual operational definition of this characteristic has been difficult because several different terms have been used in studying this phenomenon. **Repetition** has been defined as work in which a discrete set of task activities are repeated over and over in the same order without planned interruptions by other activities. A related term, **monotony**, has been used to describe the nature and impact of stimulation provided by work. Finally, a third related variable, **boredom**, is an ill-defined concept with strong emotional correlates.

No matter how repetition is defined, repetitious work has been the focus of practitioners from many fields who have been concerned with work productivity and worker satisfaction. The work conditions that resulted from the mechanization of the workplace as part of the Industrial Revolution led many practitioners to redesign jobs to alleviate their repetitious nature. This same phenomenon which has been eliminated in many blue collar jobs is now occurring in white collar jobs. Cox (1980) pointed out that the Scientific-Technological Revolution has led to repetitious job characteristics in computer-based work in white collar jobs.

To illustrate the impact that technology might have in boredom at work, read the comments below from Pam who works as an office assistant in a large corporation:

> I used to love my job. Even though I was not trained in the biochemical field, I had a chance to learn about the industry and I felt like I really added something to the work our department is doing. In the last two years we have made some changes that have cut my job down to nothing. For instance, I used to enjoy taking calls and answering questions from customers. Now that we have a voice-message system, I don't take any calls. In addition, I used to arrange and even attend training meetings we would hold for our customers. Now the company has a full-time meeting planner in the new training centre. So you see my job has been reduced to nothing. All I do is word processing projects for the scientists in the office. Many times, I don't even get to talk to the scientists. They just drop off their typing work and I return it to their mail box when I am done.

Shift Work

Having to work at times other than the traditional 9.00a.m. to 5.00p.m. day is another factor that might lead to occupational stress. The prevalence of dividing the day into two or three work shifts has increased since the First World War. Some occupations involve shift work out of social necessity. Examples of these occupations include hospitals, fire/police services and public utilities, where there is a social need to have around-the-clock coverage. Still other jobs demand shift work because of the nature of the technology that is involved. Several industries fall into this category: steel, petrochemical and paper/pulp. It is estimated that about 20 per cent of the workforce in industrialized nations are involved in some sort of shift work.

Both mental efficiency and work motivation are directly and

indirectly affected by shift work (for a complete review of physical and mental health effects, see Rutenfranz *et al.*, 1985). The difficulties associated with shift work have been explained primarily from a physiological perspective. More specifically, research has shown that human beings have a powerful timekeeping system or body clock that functions to enforce regular cycles of sleep and diurnal activity in behaviour. These cycles are called **circadian cycles** and are associated biochemically with the hormone melatonin which is suppressed when daylight levels of illumination are encountered (Monk and Tepas, 1985). In addition to these physiological effects, shift work has also been associated with psychosocial difficulties. These difficulties arise from the fact that our society is daytime orientated (Ivancevich and Matteson, 1980). Shift work might lead a worker to experience domestic pressure (for example, inability to cope with child care and household management), spousal/familial difficulties (for example, absence as social companion, sexual partner, or protector/care giver), and social isolation (for example, difficulty connecting with day working friends and making associations with certain social activities such as clubs and community groups).

Colette represents an example of an employee who experiences the stressful effects of working a shift that varies from the traditional 9.00a.m. to 5.00p.m. work day. In her work as a reservation agent for a major airline, Colette works from 12 noon until 8.00p.m. Because of her lack of seniority at the airline she has Tuesday and Wednesday as her two scheduled days off each week. She comments:

> Everyone tells me I'm lucky because I can sleep late because I don't have to be at work until noon. The reality, however, is that I don't sleep in. The rest of the world gets up at 8.00 to be at work at 9.00. In addition, I don't feel very lucky having my weekends fall in the middle of the week. The social life of my friends is structured around Friday, Saturday and Sunday. I find myself being left out of many social activities. This schedule has been tough on my social life – especially dating.

Task Attributes
A final set of job characteristics that lead to occupational stress are labelled task attributes. These are believed to affect directly and indirectly the affective and behavioural responses of an employee to a job (Turner and Lawerence, 1965). Task attributes are listed and defined in Table 4.1. Simply experiencing too much or too little of any of these attributes does not account for the stress a worker will report. Instead, an interaction between the individual

Table 4.1   *List of task attributes and definitions*

Attribute	Definition
Variety	The number of different tasks which can be prescribed for a job.
Autonomy	The amount of discretion the employee has to carry out the job.
Required interaction	The amount of necessary face-to-face communication needed to complete the tasks.
Optional interaction	The amount of voluntary face-to-face communication needed.
Knowledge and skill required	The amount of mental preparation or learning required to do the job.
Responsibility	The level of perceived accountability required for the task completion.

and the attributes represents the best explanation of perceived occupational stress.

For example, a job that offers little opportunity for interaction will be perceived as more stressful for a worker who is highly extroverted than one who is more introverted. Similarly, one worker might thrive in a job in which he or she fields a variety of technical service requests during a work day (high variety) while another worker might perceive this kind of work demand as being very stressful. Still another employee might enjoy working in a field that is constantly changing and requires continuous training in technical changes (high knowledge and skill requirements) while another employee would see this constant need for additional training as being stressful.

Thus, it appears that many of the characteristics of a job are related to occupational stress. It is important to note that some of the characteristics outlined here are unavoidable (for example, shift work in a hospital) while other characteristics might be changed (for example, offering more frequent breaks in a job that is repetitious or does not offer an opportunity for social interaction). The practitioner will need to consider this distinction in choosing among the interventions described in Chapters 6 and 7.

Interpersonal Work Relationships

The quality of relationships that employees have at work has consistently been linked to job stress (Payne, 1980). Ketz de Vries (1984) noted that at least three types of interpersonal relationships have been studied: relationships with co-workers, relationships within work groups, and relationships with supervisors/leaders.

The concept of burnout (discussed in Chapter 2) has lead to the identification of another type of interpersonal relationship that is important in understanding stress in the workplace: relationships with clients or customers. Each of these types of interpersonal relationships is discussed in this section.

Relationships with Co-workers/Work Group Relationships
In Chapter 3 the concept of social support was presented as a variable that influences how individuals deal with stress. It was suggested that having adequate social support buffers the negative effects of stress. This same concept helps explain why relationships with co-workers and within work groups are so important. Poor relationships with co-workers are associated with feelings of threat for employees. In addition, poor co-worker relationships are associated with low trust, low supportiveness and low interest/ willingness to listen and be empathic (French and Caplan, 1973). It has even been suggested that, when employees have poor relationships with co-workers, they blame the job stress they experience on their co-workers. Conversely, those workers who report the greatest amount of group cohesion are best able to cope with stress on the job (Ketz de Vries, 1984).

As an example of the impact of co-worker relationships in job-related stress, imagine the situation that might arise when two departments are merged. In one such example, two departments that had previously operated autonomously were merged into one department because of the construction of a new site where the two departments would be housed in one office. Soon after employees moved into the new space the director who managed the two departments left the organization. A new director was appointed who had previously managed one of the departments.

Because the employees in the two departments had never had an opportunity to voice their concerns about the merger, they felt as if they had been forced into a work situation that they saw as unfair. Employees in each of the two respective departments mistrusted the employees in the other department. The fact that the new director had previously worked in one of the departments left some employees believing that they would not receive fair treatment and that they would be seen as second class citizens. Any attempt at bringing the two groups together met with resistance. Joint staff meetings were disastrous and often ended in shouting matches. Eventually the director solicited the assistance of a neutral consultant to work with the group during a two day team building retreat.

It might be assumed that communication is one of the major

factors to consider in assessing relationships among co-workers. Simply talking with fellow employees may not be sufficient to improve relationships. Rather the *kind* of communication that is present seems to be important. Leiter and Maslach (1986) described two kinds of communication between co-workers: informal, socially supportive communication (for example, friendships, non-work activity) and work-related communications (for example, consultation, supervision, administration). Work-related communication is not sufficient to improve co-worker relationships; instead, informal communication that occurs between employees is most likely to alleviate job stress. Thus, informal chatter at the office coffee pot or a company picnic is very important in improving co-worker relationships.

Relationships with Supervisors

Almost anyone who works has a boss or supervisor. Just as relationships with co-workers are important in determining the amount of stress an individual experiences at work, so does the relationship an employee has with a boss or supervisor. Several aspects of this relationship have been identified as potentially affecting work-related stress. First, having 'considerate' leadership from supervisors leads employees to experience less job stress. A considerate leadership style is characterized as allowing employees to participate actively in decision making and offering an avenue for good two way communication. A great deal of research has been undertaken to understand which leadership styles are most effective in helping employees deal with job stress. These studies point to an interaction between the situation and the individual employee. In other words, the leadership style that will be most effective in helping employees deal with stress will vary across individuals and situations (Matteson and Ivancevich, 1987).

As an example, consider the difference in effective leadership styles for two groups. The first group is comprised of paramedics and fire fighters who respond to emergency rescue calls while the second group includes graphic artists who need to brainstorm creative approaches for advertising campaigns. The kinds of people working in these two groups and the kind of direction they would need to do their work would involve very different leadership styles. The employees in the fire fighter group might be accustomed to very directive leadership and even appreciate this style during emergency situations. The workers in the advertising agency, however, might see this same style as constraining creativity. Instead these employees might value a leadership style that was much more relaxed and participative in nature.

A second aspect within supervisory relationships identified as having the potential for influencing occupational stress focuses on the stress experienced by supervisors. Much discussion on job stress focuses on the stress employees feel as they deal with their supervisors. However, the behaviour of employees can lead to stress for a supervisor. Much of the work that has been done in the area of supervisory stress has been concerned with the stress that is associated with having responsibility. Ivancevich and Matteson (1980) said that supervisors are simultaneously responsible for people (the activities and work of subordinates) and for things (equipment, budgets, paperwork). This combination of responsibility can leave the supervisor vulnerable to the effects of work stress.

Consider the example of Dick who worked as an engineer for a major manufacturing company for 20 years. Because Dick was a good performer, he continued to be promoted until he eventually became superintendent of the plant where he worked. In talking with the occupational nurse at the plant, Dick shared the following comments:

> I just don't know what is wrong with me. I am short with everyone at work and at home. I'm finding it tougher to get out of bed in the morning. My wife keeps telling me that I should 'snap out' of it. She says that I should be the happiest I've ever been because I've reached the superintendent level. I know I should be happy but I am miserable. I miss being outside and doing engineering work. Who would have thought that moving into management would involve so much 'hand-holding'. I'm not cut out to sit around and listen to other people's problems.

Relationships with Clients/Customers

Still another potentially stressful relationship within the workplace is found in interactions with customers or clients. These relationships often represent the primary focus of the work an employee does. As noted in Chapter 2, the potentially stressful nature of relationships with clients has been examined in the light of occupational burnout. One group of workers who have consistently been identified as being at risk for experiencing job stress and burnout are those individuals involved in providing service to others (Schuler, 1984). For instance, as medical personnel report more contact with patients, they reported increasingly high levels of emotional exhaustion (Maslach and Jackson, 1981). Similarly, human service providers reported more feelings of helplessness as they encountered 'red tape' in dealing with organizational policies and as they worked with uncooperative clients.

Service providers may become easy targets for job stress because of the strong feelings of personal responsibility they experience in helping others and because of the infrequent feedback about work success that they receive. Consider the employee assistance programme (EAP) counsellor who works with an alcoholic employee. Because of the nature of the confidential counselling relationship, the counsellor may never know how well the employee is doing at work after the counselling relationship is terminated.

The stressors covered in this section have included relationships in a worker's immediate work environment. Stress can also be encountered from sources beyond the immediate work group. These stressors are discussed in the next section.

Organizational Structure and Climate

Most work is done in the context of an organization, and organizational behaviour and organizational development specialists have focused on the role of the organization in understanding the effects on work. In turn, a number of characteristics associated with an organization have been linked to occupational stress. In this section, four of these characteristics will be explored: organizational structure, position/level within an organization, organizational culture and organizational territory.

Organizational Structure

The potential effects of the structure of an organization on individual performance have only recently been studied and more fully understood (Ivancevich and Matteson, 1980). The extent to which individual employees are involved in direction and decision making in their work has led to the definition of two kinds of organizational structures: **centralized** organizational structure (tall organizations), in which a majority of the decision making power is placed with top-level managers and **decentralized** organizational structures (flat organizations), in which employees have more direct control of their work no matter what level they occupy in the organization. As an example of a centralized organization structure, imagine a Fortune 500 Company with 5,000 employees located throughout the world. Contrast this organizational structure with a more decentralized organizational structure with a small computer consulting company. This company is comprised of 15 employees all of whom work in one office. It would logically follow that the employees in the smaller organization would feel as if they had greater impact on the decision making that occurred in the organization.

In general, structures which allow individuals more decision making power produce less stress. For instance, Ivancevich and Donnelly (1975) studied the effects of tall, medium and flat organizational structures on employee job satisfaction and stress levels. Their result indicated that employees in flat organizations reported more job satisfaction, less job stress and better work performance. These differential effects for various organizational structures might be linked to the fact that increased decision making enhances the meaningfulness an employee finds in work and provides the employee with a greater sense of autonomy, responsibility, certainty, control and ownership (Schuler, 1980; Cooper, 1987).

Position/Level Within an Organization
A related organizational variable associated with job stress involves the position or level an individual occupies within the organization. Given the discussion of participation in decision making in the preceding section, it should not be surprising that employees who hold jobs at the low end of the organizational hierarchy are more likely to experience stress. Results from one study supported this claim. Ivancevich *et al.* (1982) compared low, middle and upper level employees on five stress variables: quantitative work overload, qualitative work overload, lack of career progression, poor supervisory relationships and role conflict. There were significant differences for groups on all of the variables, with low level employees reporting the most stress. Positions included in the low level category included middle and low level managers, operator level workers, labourers, painters, secretaries, waitresses and medical technicians.

Organizational Culture
In addition to the structure of an organization, the culture or climate has also been suggested to be a source of occupational stress. Organizations appear to have personalities shaped by top level management; in addition, the 'culture' of an organization is defined by the beliefs and expectations shared by organizational members. A particularly important stress that results from organizational culture is the existence of competition. For instance, as organizations decline, especially in relation to downsizing and budget cuts, five job stressors emerge: feelings of job insecurity, work overload because of unrealistic deadlines, underutilization of

employee skills, promotional obstacles, and intra- and intergroup competition (Jick, 1985).

Even if an organization is not experiencing cutbacks, job stress can still result from organizational culture. For instance, many workers report stress caused by power struggles or office politics. These conditions are more evident the higher an employee moves in an organization. Office politics are said to be an important factor in a number of organizational practices: promotions or transfers, allocation of supplies or equipment, division of authority and coordination between high level managers. Managers who are engaged in power games and political alliances can place stressful expectations and demands on subordinates (Matteson and Ivancevich, 1987).

Organizational Territory

A final organization characteristic linked to occupational stress involves territory. Organizational territory is defined as the personal space or arena of activities within which an employee works (Ivancevich and Matteson, 1980). Territoriality has been identified as a powerful stressor for workers (French and Caplan, 1973). To understand this concept better, consider a group of five laboratory technicians. Four of these technicians work in the main laboratory (home territory) while one of the technicians is sent to work alone in a small laboratory in another department (alien territory). The kind of stress the technician working on her own might experience would be different from the stress experienced for the group in the main laboratory. Her stress might stem from feeling alienated or isolated in the new department. However, the reverse might also be true: if there was poor group cohesion in the main laboratory, the technician might see the transfer to an alien territory as a welcome relief.

In reviewing these organizational stress variables, the practitioner might feel powerless to develop ways to intervene since changing the culture and practices of an entire organization can appear impossible. Admittedly such changes are difficult and slow to occur. There are, however, a number of stressors within the human resource management practices of an organization that can be addressed directly by practitioners. These stressors are described in the next section.

Human Resource Management Practices

Another set of potential stressors in the workplace is associated with human resource management practices. In recent years, many organizations have changed the name of the personnel function to 'human resource management' or some similar title. This name change reflects a shift in conceptualizing the human resource management function as being broader than a focus on selection and placement of employees. Today, the human resource function within many organizations includes training, career development, succession planning, compensation and benefits, outplacement, and/or affirmative action and diversity concerns.

However, this same shift in conceptualization has not necessarily occurred in the understanding of work-related stress. While most descriptions of work stress contain a cluster of career development variables, the work stress research literature does not include a comprehensive focus on how employee development within organizations is related to stress. Thus, the work-related stressors presented here include more than just stressors associated with career development; rather, we focus on all the stressors that individuals might encounter with regard to their development as employees.

Entering the Workplace
The potential for stress is great as an individual enters a new work setting (Wanous, 1969). In particular, individuals can experience stress because of the perceptual differences between what new workers expect a work environment to be like and the reality of the work environment they find. Several additional factors have been named as potential stressors at this time: dealing with ambiguity and uncertainty, concern about establishing an organizational identity, and learning to deal with managers and co-workers (Burke, 1988). Many of these stress factors have been linked to the need for adequate socialization to the new work setting. Katz (1985) reviewed the literature dealing with occupational stress and early socialization experiences and noted that having a good socialization experience (for example, through good orientation or having a supportive mentor) is consistently associated with lower levels of stress among new workers.

One major company saw the importance of helping new employees as they entered the organization. Managers from the sales division of this company received feedback that many of the sales representatives had stressful experiences after being placed alone in the field following a two week classroom training session. As a way to intervene to deal with this stress, the company implemented a new entry programme for sales personnel. The new programme involved several rotational project assignments at sales offices across the country before the representative was placed permanently and asked to work independently. At the end of each of these assignments, the new sales representatives returned to corporate headquarters for additional classroom training with a class of sales representatives who had started working at the same time. Throughout the entire programme the new sales representatives were assigned a committee of three mentors. These three mentors were senior level employees from different areas of the sales division who had no evaluatory power over the trainees and instead were available to offer support and serve as a resource to the new employees.

Lack of Training

Since training workers through workshops, seminars, apprenticeships, job rotations and continuing education is becoming commonplace in many organizations, much of the work of a human resource management department is focused on ongoing training of workers. Training is seen as being valuable because individual workers gain the psychological reward of improving themselves and organizations benefit from having workers with better skills. Training also represents a key component in the socialization of new employees. Having insufficient opportunity for training might increase the amount of uncertainty a new employee experiences, and lack of training can affect workers beyond the period when they are new in an organization. For instance, a primary stressor for older workers is in having to deal with new technology and the need for new job skills at the same time they are in competition with younger workers who have education about new technology (McGoldrick and Cooper, 1985).

Building and Maintaining a Career

A number of different stressors have been identified for individuals as they move beyond the period when they enter the workplace. These stressors are associated with the mid-career development of individuals (for example, overpromotion, underpromotion, status incongruence, thwarted ambition) (see Cooper and Marshall, 1976; Hall, 1976; London and Mone, 1987). For instance, **occupational locking-in** is a situation when people feel boxed-in because they have no ability to move from their present job or when the only job for which they are qualified is the one they already hold. As another example, consider the tension and ambiguity that individuals in mid-career feel as they attempt to balance commitments in their personal and work life. This tension may lead to a change in focus over the course of a lifetime. From the mid-20s to mid-30s, individuals focus primarily on their work and career.

During the period from the age of 35 until the early 40s, individuals are more likely to focus on private life, and finally from the early 40s into the 50s individuals come to integrate their professional and personal lives or to fragment these two areas of their lives. As we noted in Chapter 3, however, the 'fit' of this pattern to women's work experience is unclear.

As a final example of mid-career stress phenomena, Korman *et al.* (1981) described **career success and personal failure** as the strange juxtaposition that results when individuals simultaneously experience success in their career and personal/social isolation. Stress results as individuals become aware of their advancing age and mortality, career/life goals that will not be attained, decreased potential for job mobility and changes in family patterns.

As an example, consider the thoughts of Carlos who is 50 years old and works as an accountant for a large company:

> When I started working things were different. You didn't even talk about your personal life in relation to work. So I did what I was supposed to. I went to work and worked very hard; never asking questions and always assuming that the company would take care of me if I did good work. Well they have taken care of me in terms of promotions but what they couldn't take care of is what I've missed in terms of my family. My two oldest children are in college and ready to move on with their own lives. My youngest daughter will go to college next year and I feel like my job has made me miss watching them grow up. Even my wife has gone on with her life. She went back to school and has finished her degree. If she lands a teaching job she will be busy with her own work and where will that leave me.

Performance Feedback

Still another area where occupational stress is linked to human resource management is performance feedback. It has long been known that receiving feedback can enhance performance and motivation; similarly, absence of feedback can represent a potential occupational stressor. Two dimensions have been identified in understanding the association between job stress and performance feedback. First, it has been suggested that a faulty feedback system can lead to occupational stress. Consider the use of an evaluation form that does not give clear behavioural examples of performance and includes a rating on 'initiative'. This evaluation system might prove stressful for an employee who does not understand that the low rating she received on initiative is related to the fact that her manager does not see her making phone calls to generate new accounts for the firm.

The second dimension related to stress is concerned with the frequency with which an individual receives feedback. As might be expected, the less frequently a worker receives direct feedback about performance, the more likely the worker is to experience stress. As an example, consider the new employee who, having recently graduated from college, is accustomed to receiving performance feedback almost immediately each time an exam, paper or project is completed. This same individual might experience stress when he begins working for an organization and finds he receives formal feedback only once each year during his performance review.

Rewards

Employees also experience stress in relation to the rewards they receive for doing work. If workers feel they are not being adequately rewarded for performance, they are likely to encounter stress. In part, rewards for performance include the traditional monetary compensation and benefits that are administered within the human resource management function in organizations. In addition, however, stress might result if employees feel they are not receiving adequate informal rewards. Such rewards might involve special treatment, privilege, recognition, or 'perks'.

One manager worked as the director of a student service department at a college. She commented on the stress that she experiences when she cannot pay her employees more money as managers are allowed to do in business. She said she would spend endless hours trying to find non-monetary rewards to motivate her employees. Finally, feeling as if she had exhausted all possibilities, she shared the dilemma with the employees in her department. She reports being surprised by the results:

> I was pleasantly surprised by what happened. I held individual meetings with all five people in my department. First I was happy to learn that all of the employees understood that monetary rewards were not likely in an academic institution. Secondly, I was pleased to find that each of the employees could easily identify rewards that would keep them motivated. For instance, one counsellor said she saw reward in being able to take on one new project each semester. Another said she would stay motivated by being able to change job responsibilities every few years. Still another employee indicated that being allowed extra time for professional development would serve as a great reward for him.

Job Future Ambiguity and Insecurity

Another area of concern for human resource management practitioners is the potential stress that arises when workers feel uncertain about the security of their jobs. In recent years, there has been a change in traditional organizational structures (for example, downsizing, right sizing, elimination of middle management, self-managed work teams). These changes have meant that formerly secure jobs (especially management and professional jobs) are no longer as likely to assure employees of long-term employment. Three factors have led to these changes and the subsequent stress for workers: an increase in the number of organizational acquisitions and mergers; an increase in competition for jobs because younger people come to the workplace with better education than the older workers have; and the continuing introduction of new technology which leaves many workers with obsolete skills (Hunt and Hunt, 1983). In addition, a 'ripple effect' occurs in the stress that employees experience with regard to job insecurity. Not only do those workers who actually lose their jobs experience stress, but stress also occurs among individuals who see one co-worker lose a job and in turn begin to worry about their own security (Greenhalgh and Rosenblatt, 1984).

One employee describes the stress that was experienced in one work group after lay-offs were announced:

> This whole place feels like stress. It's like being on an emotional roller coaster. On the one hand you feel relieved that you weren't terminated but on the other hand you feel guilt and sadness for co-workers who do not have jobs any more. These aren't just numbers on the 6.00 news anymore; they're my friends, people who I see around town, people who have families like me. I also feel panic – wondering if the company will do it again. I have to wonder if I'll be next. I'm also angry. So the company has cut costs by letting people go. What does that mean for me? More work. Just because there are fewer people doesn't mean the work is still not here. This whole thing is a mess – it's no way to work.

Job/Career Transitions
Having to make a change or transition of any sort can be stressful, and transitions in one's work are not an exception. The kinds of transitions that individuals make in work might result from a change in job, profession, or orientation towards work (for example, beginning to work part-time because of maternity leave). These transitions can be stressful because of the changes an individual must make in work and in life outside of work. As noted in Chapter 1, even positive transitions (such as a promotion) can lead to stress. For instance, transition as seemingly simple as job rotation within the same department can lead to stress as an individual might feel uncertain, helpless and afraid of unknown work demands (Ketz de Vries, 1984).

Leaving the Workforce

A special case of transition occurs when a worker leaves the workforce, and a number of stressors have been identified when an individual ends a career or prepares to retire. These stressors involve the psychological, physiological and social areas of a person's life. Such stressors might include dealing with the ageing process, facing changes in physical and mental abilities, coping with new technology and skill obsolescence, confronting the reality of lack of promotions and preparing for retired life.

Physical Qualities and Technology

To this point, all of the stressors identified in this taxonomy of work setting variables have been primarily psychological in nature. The remaining category of stressors is directly related to the physical work environment. The physical qualities of work stress are defined as the physical conditions that surround an individual. Stress occurs with regard to physical variables when a minimum level of biological functioning and physical safety is not maintained. The potentially stressful physical qualities of work have often been labelled 'blue collar stressors' because they are most often observed in work settings where blue collar workers are employees (Poulton, 1978). A list of some of the stressors associated with the physical environment are outlined in Table 4.2 (for a more complete discussion of these variables, see Ivancevich and Matteson, 1980; Kelly and Cooper, 1981; Wallace *et al.*, 1988).

In reviewing the stressors in Table 4.2, it is obvious that there are negative physical consequences associated with the stressors. For example, exposure to excessive noise can lead to deafness. There is however, more subtle psychological stress associated with some of the stressors. As described in Chapter 1 in our discussion of Selye's model, humans experience stress when they cannot cope with their environment. As an example, heat has been linked to increased irritability while cold is associated with decreased motivation (Ivancevich and Matteson, 1980).

Stressors in the physical work environment are not limited to blue collar jobs. While management or professional jobs usually do not involve exposure to hazardous or noxious agents, they can include physical stressors. Consider the trading floor of a large commodities firm, filled with 80 people, all screaming. On the wall are 10 large clocks that show the time in major cities around the world. Background noise includes ringing telephones, telex operators yelling quotients and rows of traders shouting market prices (Matteson and Ivancevich, 1987). Other stressors found in

Table 4.2 *Physical stressors in the work environment*

Physical stressor	Examples
Light	Insufficient lighting in a workshop.
	Excessive glare in a laboratory.
	Psychological quality in an office (e.g. cheerfulness).
Noise	Continued exposure to loud machinery.
	Interruption by loud noise in an office.
Temperature	Extreme cold in outdoor construction.
	Extended exposure to heat in a manufacturing plant.
	Fluctuations in temperature in an office.
Vibration and motion	Operating equipment (e.g. jackhammer).
	Riding a machine (e.g. forklift).
Polluted air	Breathing toxic fumes in a processing laboratory.
	Exposure to pathogenic agent through the skin in a chemical plant.
	Exposure to radiation during a nuclear power plant accident.
Ergonomic factors	Excessive muscular workload in a lumber yard.
	High sensory demand at the control board in an airplane cockpit.
	Machine paced work on an assembly line.

the work environments of white collar workers include crowding (Suedfeld, 1979), lack of privacy (Cohen, 1980), background colour (Jokl, 1984) and working on computer video terminals (Chadrow, 1984).

Another area related to the physical environment that has been suggested as potentially stressful is technology. Technology is defined as the way an organization transforms research and other inputs into desirable outputs. Several specific stressors associated with technology have been identified. For instance, **technical limitations** may lead to stress (Woodward, 1965). Imagine a laboratory technician working on a chemical process that necessitates taking chemical readings every hour for 24 hours. If no technology exists to obtain the readings without human involvement, the laboratory technician will be forced to find a way to have a person available around the clock to take the readings.

Similarly, **technical arrangement** might also be related to job stress. More specifically, the technical arrangement within a work environment refers to the way processes, equipment and people are linked by technology. As a simplistic example, consider a human resource agency that becomes involved in tracking service delivery using a computer database. To use the database system effectively, the entire staff (counsellors, secretaries and managers) must agree on the variables that will be tracked by the system and the method by which data will be gathered and recorded. In addition, the staff would need to work with computer experts to design the system. Stress might develop for workers in this example because of the mix of occupations, skill levels, management styles and task attributes.

Schuler (1977) describes another technology-based stressor related to the amount of congruence between technology, task attributes and organizational structure, termed **task–technology-structure fit**. Stress will be least significant in situations where technology is constructed to match the way the work group is organized and the nature of the tasks. In a study with an engineering division of a public utility, Schuler found that role ambiguity stress was lowest in situations in which the task–technology–structure fit was most congruent.

Technology design represents another source of potential stress in work settings. For instance, Otway and Misenta (1980) suggested that the design of a control room can enhance stress. The researchers noted that had the control room at the Three Mile Island nuclear plant been designed using more sophisticated ergonomic principles, the accident might not have occurred. Similarly, Ostberg and Nilsson (1985) pointed out that role overload and role underload can result from the design of a control room. More specifically, they described a situation in which a control room is designed to operate without any human interaction when the system is functioning properly, thus resulting in role underload as a worker becomes bored. If the system malfunctions, the design of the control room necessitates more work than the single worker can perform (role overload).

Summary

Stress factors associated with the workplace that have been described here include many aspects of the job. In particular, variables associated with stress in the workplace range from the individual worker, to the immediate work environment, and even to the entire organization. However, many of these factors can be changed through effective interventions, the design and implementation of which are the focus of Chapters 6 and 7.

5
Individual Interventions

To this point in this book, we have presented information about causes of occupational stress. With this information as a foundation, we now turn to topics that are the focus of the remainder of the book: designing interventions for dealing with occupational stress (Chapters 5, 6 and 8) and methods for evaluating the effectiveness of those interventions (Chapter 7). In describing the factors that are associated with occupational stress, we divided them into categories (individual characteristics, workplace variables). Our discussion of interventions will also be divided into categories. The present chapter will focus on interventions that can be undertaken to help an individual cope with stress; Chapter 6 will describe interventions designed to change the workplace to reduce job stress.

It should be noted that these two categories of interventions are not mutually exclusive. For example, a practitioner might plan an organization-wide programme to teach relaxation methods to employees. Thus, a strategy for helping individuals cope with stress could be used to affect the entire organization. For better understanding of how a practitioner might design a comprehensive intervention programme, however, these two types of interventions are described separately. In particular, the interventions described in this chapter focus on ways that an individual might cope with the effects of stress. These interventions can occur at or away from work and may target eliminating or reducing the source of discomfort, altering one's appraisal of the stressor, or managing and reducing the feelings of discomfort within the individual (Murphy, 1985).

The key component to understanding how these individual responses affect stress is **coping**, a concept described in Chapter 1. Coping was generally defined as ways that people respond to stressors. There are many examples of ways that people use to cope with stress, some of which are unhealthy. For example, consider the worker who eats 'junk' food, smokes cigarettes and drinks alcohol as a means of coping with stress at work. Stress management interventions are designed to teach workers healthy coping strategies to deal with work-related stress. The goal of these interventions is for individuals to learn new coping skills that improve their ability to manage their environment and reduce their stress.

Just as the term 'stress' is difficult to define, 'stress management' has come to summarize a wide variety of techniques and strategies. The many interventions associated with stress management can make it difficult for a practitioner to decide which intervention might be most appropriate for a given individual. One method of categorizing these interventions is to consider the way in which any particular strategy helps the individual to cope with stress. In an extensive review of stress management research Mathney *et al.* (1986) grouped stress management interventions into two categories: **preventive coping**, responses to alleviate stress as it is initially perceived, and **combative coping**, strategies for combating stressors already underway. Further, Mathney *et al.* proposed classes of strategies associated with each of the two types of coping. These classes are listed in Table 5.1.

Table 5.1   *Classes of coping strategies*

Coping strategy	Classes
Combative	Avoiding stressors through life adjustments or adjusting demand levels. Altering stress-inducing behaviour patterns. Developing coping resources.
Preventive	Monitoring stressors and symptoms. Marshalling resources and attacking stressors. Tolerating unavoidable stressors. Lowering stressful arousal.

This outline will be used in this chapter to describe individual intervention strategies so that the practitioner can select different strategies depending on the 'diagnosis' of the stressful situation that confronts the individual worker. It should be noted, however, that defining an intervention strategy as *either* preventive or combative is not always clear cut. In fact, some strategies might be *both* preventive and combative. For example, learning assertiveness skills may combat a stressful relationship with a co-worker and prevent future problems with a supervisor. For purposes of discussion here, each of the coping strategies will be labelled *primarily* preventive or combative. The intervention strategies to be described in this chapter are listed in Table 5.2.

Table 5.2 *Intervention strategies*

Primarily preventive	Primarily combative
Monitoring stressors and symptoms	Developing coping resources
• stress diaries	• social support
• muscle monitoring	• time management
• tension thermometer	Altering stress-inducing behaviour patterns
Marshalling resources and attacking stressors	• Type A Behaviour Pattern
	Avoiding stressors through adjustment
• social skills training	• family/work balance
• assertive training	• career planning
• problem solving skills training	
Tolerating stressors	
• cognitive appraisal	
• cognitive restructuring	
• cognitive rehearsal	
• stress inoculation training	
Lowering arousal	
• deep breathing	
• progressive muscle relaxation (PMR)	
• transcendental meditation (TM)	
• Benson technique	
• diagnostic meditation (DM)	
• autogenic suggestion	
• self-hypnosis	
• guided imagery	
• yoga	
• biofeedback	
• physical exercise	

Preventive Strategies

Monitoring Stressors and Symptoms

One strategy for helping individuals cope with stress involves focusing on the signs and symptoms of stress. This strategy is labelled preventive because we believe that individuals can avoid stress if they become aware of events or symptoms that lead to a stress reaction. Several specific techniques have been suggested.

One technique is requiring individuals to keep a **stress diary** which is a personal record or log of events that happen before a negative stress response (Ivancevich and Matteson, 1980). Different variations of format might be used. For instance, the stress log might ask individuals to make an entry every time they encounter a stressful event. The entry would include a specific description of the event along with a description of the feelings and thoughts that resulted from the event. An alternative format is illustrated in Table 5.3. Using this stress log format, a practitioner could ask the individual to make an entry at each of

Table 5.3   *Weekly stress log*

DAY:	MON	TUES	WED	THUR	FRI	SAT	SUN
TIME:							
A.M.							
Time:							
Symptoms:							
Activity/event:							
NOON:							
Time:							
Symptoms:							
Activity/event:							
P.M.							
Time:							
Symptoms:							
Activity/event:							

Examples of symptoms:

Headaches	Sweating	Diarrhoea
Nervousness	No energy	Sore muscles
Shaky inside	Confusion	Stiff neck
Critical of others	Blaming yourself	Nausea
Difficulty remembering	Backaches	Worrying
Chest pains	Constipation	Weakness

several specified times during the day. For each entry, the individual would note the stress symptoms that are occurring and the activities or events that might be causing the symptoms. This format is especially useful for individuals who have trouble identifying the kinds of stress symptoms they experience or the events that lead to stress.

No matter which format is used, there are two important cautions for the stress diary technique. First, the practitioner must encourage the individual to be serious about keeping the log for an extended period of time (that is, several weeks). This encouragement is especially important for highly stressed individuals who might say they are 'too busy' to deal with their stress. Second, the practitioner should help the individual analyse the results of the stress diary. This analysis might focus on identifying themes or patterns that point to specific kinds of stress responses in relation to specific events. In turn, these patterns can then be used in planning other interventions.

After reviewing the results of a stress log that was kept by a manager of a computer programming department, one counsellor arrived at these conclusions and suggested interventions.

Observation	Intervention
Symptoms of stress seem to be physical in nature – especially muscle tension.	Review progressive muscle relaxation exercises with employee.
Many stress reactions are preceded by meetings with the employee's boss.	Explore the relationship the employee has with the boss and develop strategies to improve the relationship.
Consistent pattern of not completing work that was planned for a given day.	Discuss time management skills and whether the daily goals being set are realistic.

Muscle Monitoring

A related technique involves monitoring muscular tension that occurs as a result of stress. Classic tension symptoms of stress include a sore jaw, tense neck, or aching back, symptoms that are obviously the result of clenching or tightening specific muscle groups in response to stressful situations. These reactions might be described using the stress response of the general adaptation syndrome (GAS) outlined in Chapter 1. While these responses are effective in coping with stress in the short run, the long-term effects are harmful.

Several specific techniques for monitoring muscle tension have been presented. One method for increasing awareness of variations in physical tension is by introducing individuals to the use of a hypothetical measuring instrument, the **tension thermometer** (Roskies, 1987). Each person is encouraged to develop his or her own anchor points on a scale from 1 to 10 to denote a tension state. Then, individuals use the scale to report their level of tension at various points in time to see when changes in tension have occurred. Another suggested muscle monitoring technique is to associate paying attention to muscle states with some reoccurring event. For example, every time the phone rings or an individual leaves his or her desk, the individual is instructed to become aware of body tension and then to relax.

Chapter 8 includes sample materials that might be used in educating employees about the general nature of stress and how humans respond physically and psychologically to stressful situations. These sample materials include general information and a series of checklists and inventories. In working with individuals, practitioners might be surprised to learn that even though employees claim they 'know all there is to know about stress', they are often better able to cope if they understand conceptually how stress affects them. In addition, many employees benefit from taking time to identify the specific stressors and symptoms that cause them the most difficulty in their work.

Practitioners will need to be creative in devising ways of delivering this information to employees. If a practitioner has the luxury of doing one-to-one counselling with an employee, these techniques can be tailored to fit the exact needs of an individual. Often, however, one-to-one counselling sessions are not realistic. There are other ways to share this information with employees. For instance in one organization, an employee assistance programme (EAP) counsellor writes a column in the company newsletter, covering different topics each month. Another human resource management employee has organized a lunch-time series of stress talks. He has found speakers from within the organization and the local community to do these presentations. In another company, a nurse from the medical department has worked with the communication department to produce a video on stress topics that can be viewed by employees and that is broadcast on television monitors throughout the corporation's headquarters.

The techniques described in this section involve passive attention to effects that stress might have on an individual. The rationale for these strategies is that simply becoming aware of the symptoms of stress may be sufficient in increasing coping or reducing stress. In the next section, a set of more active preventive strategies are presented which involve marshalling resources and attacking stressors.

Marshalling Resources and Attacking Stressors
Another set of interventions useful in preventing stress involves developing skills which prepare individuals to cope with stressful situations as they occur. Several specific strategies that fit this category include training in social skills and problem solving, skills that will help individuals cope with social interactions that may lead to stress. A practitioner who is dealing with an individual lacking skills in one of these areas might point out how developing these skills will prevent stressful situations from occurring or reoccurring.

As a response to the stress an individual might experience from social anxiety, researchers have developed interventions aimed at **social skills training**. A wide variety of behaviours are included under this heading, but, in general, these strategies focus on developing skills to help an individual interact more easily with other people. Jaremko (1983) developed a training programme for socially anxious individuals to deal with five response categories: initiating and maintaining conversation, making and refusing requests, giving and receiving criticism, giving and receiving compliments, and interpreting non-verbal cues in the behaviour of others. Participants in such a programme would view videotapes of appropriate and inappropriate behaviour in each area, role-play the skills, receive feedback on their behaviour, and complete homework assignments on the skills they are learning.

A special subset of social skills training is **assertiveness training**. Training in this area leads to skills that help individuals respond in a straightforward manner with regard to what they believe, feel and want in the world (Mathney *et al.*, 1986). As an example of how assertiveness training might work, consider Alice who works as a secretary. She seeks assistance because she has become so frustrated with the large number of last minute requests she has received for typing in recent weeks that she 'blew up' and threw a stack of papers at her boss. The counsellor working with Alice could help her see how more assertive communication earlier in the process might have diffused the emotions that eventually led to her erratic behaviour.

In particular, work with Alice might include helping her to distinguish between passive, aggressive and assertive communication styles. In addition, the counsellor might examine irrational beliefs that Alice has about being assertive (such as, 'It's not okay to say no; If I speak up, others won't like me') and substitute more adaptive ones for these beliefs (such as, 'If I decline a request, my boss might be disappointed but she will still value me as a person'). Finally, the counsellor might model and role play verbal and non-verbal behaviour to help Alice communicate more assertively. For instance, the counsellor might get Alice to practise asking to see her boss and saying 'When I receive last minute requests for typing, I feel frustrated and angry. To avoid a situation like the one that occurred last week, I would like to see if there is a way for you to anticipate in advance when you will have requests for typing.' A sample agenda and copies of materials designed to teach these assertiveness skills are included in Chapter 8.

The comments that Alice made to her boss describe another set of skills that can be taught to prevent stress: **problem solving skills**. These skills help an individual respond with some action that will reduce the stressfulness of a situation. A practitioner can teach individuals or groups of workers to develop skills that will help them to be more creative or proactive in reaching solutions to potentially stressful problems. One useful training programme in this area was developed at the Harvard Negotiation Project (Fisher and Ury, 1981). This training programme encourages participants to move beyond traditional negotiating strategies in which each person sees the other as an enemy and both parties 'dig in their heels' to do battle. Instead, the system teaches skills that focus on the issue to be solved, not the people involved, and that invent options which represent mutual gains for both parties.

An example of application of effective negotiation skills is seen in this conversation between an employee and a supervisor. Notice how the focus of problem solving is on filling needs and not winning a position.

Supervisor: I've made a decision, there will be no 'flex-time' in this office.

Employee: I understand you've made a decision – but can I ask what led you to that decision?

Supervisor: Well, I need someone to be available to answer phones and field walk-in requests during regular business hours. You and Pat are the only two available to fill these roles.

Employee: So if we could find a way to cover phones and walk-ins you would be satisfied?

Supervisor: Yes, I think so.

Employee: Well, Pat and I have devised a system where I would work early 6.30–3.30 and Pat would work late 9.30–6.30. Thus the phones would be covered during regular business hours and we could even expand our hours for accounts on the East and West coasts. Also, it would meet our family needs of sharing day care responsibilities with our spouses.

Supervisor: Sounds fair – but I am anxious about making decisions that are final.

Employee: What if we try this system for two months and then meet to decide if it is working?

The strategies presented in this section lead to the development of skills that help individuals prevent stress because of good communications. There are, however, times when negative and stressful situations are inevitable. The next section describes interventions that help individuals use coping responses that involve tolerating stressors in a way that reduces their stressful effects.

Tolerating Stressors

In describing stress in Chapter 1, we noted that encountering stress in life is inevitable. Given this reality, interventions can help individuals tolerate stressors by altering the way particular stressors are viewed (primary and secondary appraisal in Lazarus' terms). These interventions are grouped under one general heading,

cognitive-behavioural techniques, because they focus on the thoughts and actions a person has in relation to stress. The theoretical conceptualizations underlying these techniques are quite simple. In fact, Kendall and Bemis (1983) suggested that cognitive-behavioural techniques include four basic guiding principles:

1 Individuals do not respond directly to their environment; they respond to their own cognitive interpretation of the environment.
2 Cognitions (thoughts), emotions (feelings) and behaviours (actions) are causally interrelated.
3 The prediction and understanding of negative cognitions and behaviours are enhanced by paying attention to a person's expectancies, beliefs and attributions.
4 It is possible and desirable to combine and integrate cognitive approaches to correcting problems with performance-based and behavioural contingency management.

One cognitive-behavioural technique is **cognitive appraisal**, also called perspective taking (Matteson and Ivancevich, 1987). This technique involves teaching individuals to assess the severity of a stressor by considering the perspective in which they view a particular stressful situation. More specifically, individuals are encouraged to ask themselves certain questions when a negative event is encountered. If a worker is frustrated with a co-worker who misses an important deadline, the worker would ask himself if the missed deadline will matter in five years, one year, one month, one week, or one day. Similarly, the worker might appraise the event by asking himself about the consequences of the event: 'What is the worst possible outcome of missing this deadline?' In this case, the worker would see that the error will not pose a threat to his life or job security but instead will result in extra work or an apology to a customer. In addition, the worker might gain a new perspective by considering if any positive results might be associated with the negative event (for example, having missed the deadline, we will be allowed more time to produce a quality product; or missing this deadline points to a need for our work group to assess how we communicate about timelines).

A related cognitive-behavioural technique is **cognitive restructuring**. This technique is based on the premise that many people believe other people or events outside of themselves are responsible for how they feel. The resulting beliefs can be irrational and quite often lead to increased stress. Thus, the aim of this technique is to help individuals cope with stress by changing their beliefs or cognitions. One model that has been proposed to understand this relationship is the A-B-C model where A represents the activating event and C denotes the consequences (feelings and behaviours) that occur in relation to the activating event. Cognitive restructuring concerns changing the B component of the model, the beliefs that occur *between* the activating event and the consequences. As an example, consider an employee who has an encounter with a rude customer (activating event) and in turn feels angry or raises her voice (consequence).

Using cognitive restructuring, a practitioner could help the employee see that it is not necessarily the customer's behaviour that leads to the dysfunctional behaviour but instead that her thoughts and beliefs mediated the response. The employee might see that the beliefs she holds (for example, because I am polite to people, they should be polite in return) will lead to increased stress because she cannot control the behaviour of others. Restructuring the thought would lead the employee to substitute a more rational belief (for example, I am not responsible for the behaviour of this customer; or this customer's rudeness is not related to my behaviour but to frustration with the situation). Matteson and Ivancevich (1987) noted the importance of keeping in mind that the objective of cognitive restructuring is not to magically make people feel good about unpleasant events. Rather, the goal is to tolerate stressors by replacing negative feelings with neutral ones, or at least less negative ones. Sample materials for teaching these techniques are included in Chapter 8.

Cognitive appraisal and cognitive restructuring are designed to help people tolerate stressors after they occur. A related technique, **cognitive rehearsal**, involves helping people tolerate stressors by anticipating them before they happen. This technique calls for visualizing a potentially stressful event before it occurs and practising or rehearsing how to respond, a rehearsal that should occur while the individual is relaxed and might include appraisal or restructuring as outlined above (Matteson and Ivancevich, 1987). Consider an employee who finds annual performance reviews very stressful. This employee might rehearse how he or she will respond in advance.

As an example of this technique, consider the following dialogue between a counsellor and an employee:

> *Counsellor*: Were you able to identify some thoughts that you can rehearse before you go into your performance review?
> *Employee*: Yes I came up with three: I know I am a valued employee; I know my job is secure; the feedback my boss is offering is supposed to help me improve.

Counsellor: Excellent. Did you come up with any other techniques to help you deal with the stress?

Employee: Yes. Based on our discussion last week, I thought it might be worthwhile to ask my boss to identify areas that she sees as strengths for me.

Stress inoculation training is a technique that combines all of the techniques outlined above. Developed by Meichenbaum (1977), stress inoculation training focuses on altering the way an individual processes information about a stressful situation and identifies cognitive and behavioural coping skills to change unproductive ways of reacting (Ivancevich and Matteson, 1988). The training includes three stages summarized in Table 5.4. This approach has been used to help people deal with a wide variety of stress reactions including anger, anxiety and fear.

Table 5.4 *Stages of Meichenbaum's stress inoculation training*

Stage	Description
1 Preparation	Educating the individual about the relationship between maladaptive thoughts and behaviour patterns and convincing the individual that he or she is not helpless in coping with stress situations.
2 Skill training	Helping the individual confront stressful situations by using coping skills that he or she already has or by developing new coping skills.
3 Application training	Getting the individual to practise and apply newly developed skills. For some individuals, this might involve gradually increasing the intensity of the stress to which an individual is exposed.

As an example of a potential application of this intervention, consider Sara who had an intense fear of speaking in front of groups. Because her job required her to make presentations on a regular basis, her anxiety reactions before she spoke severely affected her performance. Using some of the principles from stress inoculation training, Sara worked with an EAP counsellor to examine the negative messages she gave herself about speaking in front of groups. In addition, she learned relaxation techniques that could be used as she prepared to make a presentation.

In particular, the counsellor helped Sara develop the following list of coping messages to deal with her speech anxiety:

1 I know the material that I need to present and it will come to me easily when I speak.

2 I have spent sufficient time preparing for the presentation to have success.

3   I have had success at giving presentations in the past and can do well again.
4   The people in the session are not here to evaluate my speaking style but are interested in the material I have to share.
5   Some amount of anxiety is normal when people make presentations.
6   If I begin to feel nervous, I can cope with these symptoms by breathing deeply and relaxing.

The techniques presented in this section improve the means by which an individual can tolerate stressors by focusing on the relationship between thoughts and actions. These techniques serve as powerful tools in assisting employees to recognize that they can help control stress reactions by changing their thinking. In the next section, we examine a final set of preventive coping strategies. Unlike techniques aimed at cognitions, the techniques in the next section involve concentrating on physiological response to stress.

Lowering Arousal
In Chapter 1, we described several models of how humans respond to stress. These models suggest that the human body prepares itself to respond to stress by changing certain bodily functions (such as, heart rate, blood flow, muscle tension). It was also noted that these physiological changes can lead to stress symptoms if they are prolonged. Thus, a final set of interventions to help individuals prevent the negative effects of stress are techniques that involve lowering physiological arousal.

One of the simplest, yet most useful, techniques for lowering physiological arousal is **deep breathing**. With this technique, individuals receive instruction on how to breathe more deeply, avoiding shallow (thoracic) breaths that are often associated with the stress response and instead breathing from the abdomen. Physiological arousal is affected by this technique because of the close association between the breathing centre and the reticular activating system (RAS) in the brain. The RAS controls neuro-muscular functioning and, thus, deep breathing leads to relaxation in the neuro-muscular system (Matteson and Ivancevich, 1987). Teaching people the technique of deep breathing to increase relaxation has met with great success. In a review of the literature, Mason (1980) reported very positive results for interventions involving deep breathing. Instructions for teaching a variety of deep breathing techniques are included in Chapter 8.

An extension of deep breathing is **progressive muscle relaxation** (PMR), a technique developed by Jacobson (1938). With PMR, an individual is instructed to assume a comfortable position and to begin to breathe deeply. Then, the individual relaxes groups of muscles one at a time, beginning with the muscles in the feet, the legs, etc. Jacobson proposed that the mind 'relaxes' using this technique because relaxed muscles are associated with a decrease in emotional tension. Just as with deep breathing, PMR can be taught but full development of the skill takes practice. Jacobson recommended practising the skill two times per day for 15 to 20 minute sessions. Eventually the skill is learned so well that an individual can achieve complete muscle relaxation very quickly.

Deep breathing and muscle relaxation form the foundation for several other techniques aimed at lowering arousal. The technique of **meditation**, for instance, includes several ways to redirect mental processes away from daily life (for a complete review, see Sethi, 1984a). Meditation is defined as a non-calculating mood that occurs spontaneously or with the aid of some technique that leads to an altered state of consciousness free from tension, anxiety, or distress. Forms of meditation are used by people universally. Simply listening to music or watching a sunset can be examples of meditation (Ivancevich and Matteson, 1980). However, several more advanced forms of meditation have been developed.

Transcendental meditation (TM) is a technique that stems from Eastern culture and philosophy. The technique calls for assuming a comfortable position and concentrating on a special word called a 'mantra' (a Sanskrit word meaning sacred counsel). The altered state associated with TM is achieved when physical and mental relaxation are at a peak. This technique can be taught in four lessons given over four days by a TM instructor (Matteson and Ivancevich, 1987). Another meditation technique was developed by Benson (1975) at the Harvard Medical School. The **Benson technique** is similar to TM in that individuals assume a comfortable position and begin deep breathing through the nose. Then individuals focus passive attention on a single word, although not a secret word as is the mantra in TM. Benson proposed that using this technique summons forth a state labelled the 'relaxation response', said to be the opposite of the body's response to stress (see Table 5.5). A final type of meditation, **diagnostic meditation** (DM), is described by Sethi (1984b). DM combines several meditation systems and also includes other stress management interventions such as time management, problem solving and bio-feedback. With this technique, an individual focuses on a specific goal or situation and then, using meditation and relaxation, develops ways to reach the goal.

The basic building blocks of these meditation systems, including

Table 5.5   *Elements of the relaxation response*

Relaxation is a form of meditation – a state of concentration. By using the mind to focus upon an object, image, or thought, one cancels out all distraction associated with everyday life. The 'relaxation response' is induced to counter balance the stress response.
There are four basic elements of the 'relaxation response':

1   A quiet environment – to turn off external distractions.
2   A comfortable position – sitting or kneeling with back straight – no tight clothing.
3   An object, thought, or image to dwell upon (repetition of a word or sound such as 'one', focusing upon breathing, or saying, 'I am relaxed').
4   A passive attitude – allowing an emptying of distracting thoughts.

Relaxation *is not*:

1   A loss of control.
2   A loss of consciousness.
3   A state of sleep.
4   A state of drowsiness.

With regular practice once or twice a day for 10–15 minutes, the following results are possible:

During relaxation you will experience:
1   A decrease in the rate of metabolism, a restful state with a drop in heart rate and respiratory rate.
2   A marked decrease in the body's oxygen consumption.
3   A decrease in blood pressure.
4   A decrease in muscle tension.

After relaxation, you may notice carry over effects including:
1   Lower response to stress – less anxiety.
2   Better coping abilities.
3   A new found acceptance of self, more tolerant of own weaknesses or limitations.
4   Improved learning ability, better retention and recall.
5   A sense of calm, of being collected – a more quiet, philosophical attitude.

the relaxation response, are the same for several other techniques: **autogenic suggestion, self hypnosis, guided imagery** and **yoga**. In a review of the literature on meditation and relaxation techniques Kuna (1975) reported these techniques had positive effects on work adjustment, work performance, job satisfaction and anxiety.

A sample agenda of how these techniques could be included in one training programme is given in Table 5.6. The advantage of these techniques is that they can be learned and used in a variety of settings, including the workplace. Practitioners could obviously work with individual employees to teach these techniques. In addition some practitioners have offered education in these techniques using several other formats. For instance in one organization, written materials and audiotapes are available for employees

Table 5.6   *Suggested agenda for relaxation training*

Session	Topics to be covered
1	Introduction to course. Discuss the relaxation response. Teach breathing techniques.
2	Review homework. Review quick techniques for relaxation. Introduce progressive muscle relaxation (PMR). Assign PMR practice.
3	Review progress on PMR. Introduce guided imagery. Assign continued PMR practice.
4	Review progress on PMR. Conduct guided imagery exercise. Assign guided imagery practice.
5	Review progress on guided imagery exercises. Discuss other uses of guided imagery. Assign continued practice.
6	Review course content. Discuss exercise and overall wellness plan. Introduce personal action plan and allow participants to create their own plan. Evaluate the course.

to practise relaxation skills at home. One company has even set up a relaxation room where employees can go during the work day. This room provides a quiet environment and tapes with headphones that employees can use for listening to relaxation tapes.

Biofeedback as a stress management technique grew out of work in several fields, including psychology and physiology. In psychology, for instance, work with laboratory animals in operant conditioning studies led to the discovery that animals could be trained to control certain autonomic bodily functions. This work was extended to humans, where it was found that receiving immediate feedback or information on physiological factors could lead to individuals learning to control visceral parameters including brain waves, heart rate, muscle tension, body temperature, stomach acidity and blood pressure. Using this methodology, biofeedback has been involved in treating disease and in decreasing physiological responses associated with stress. Since the bodily functions that are the target of biofeedback are not detectable, special equipment is used to alert the individuals to physiological changes (for example, a change in tone pitch or light intensity). To monitor these changes sensors are attached to the body. The most common of these sensors are electrical sensors used to detect myocardial activity, muscle tension and brain wave activity. Similarly, transducers are used to measure blood flow and photoplelhysmographs are used to measure pulse pressure (Matteson and Ivancevich, 1987). Two different types of biofeedback have been developed. **Operant conditioning** biofeedback involves using physiological information as a reinforcer to bring about the desired physiological changes. **Augmented** biofeedback is more commonly used as a stress management technique and involves providing the individual with continuous feedback about physiological functioning (Brown, 1984).

Use of biofeedback has been shown to be effective in helping individuals restore their bodies to non-stressed states. In one study, a group of employees who suffered from chronic tension headaches and chronic anxiety at Equitable Life Insurance Company were given nine weeks of biofeedback training. After the training individuals reported a 50 per cent reduction in headaches and a significant decrease in the interference of stress-related symptoms (Matteson and Ivancevich, 1987). However, other studies have not found such significantly positive results. For example, in reviewing studies on biofeedback, Stoney *et al.* (1987) concluded that there is no scientific support for the effectiveness of biofeedback in treating stress-related problems. Another criticism of biofeedback as a stress management technique is that it is costly in the time involved in instructing individuals and in the kinds of equipment that are required. Thus, some critics have argued that money and effort might be better spent on more conventional stress management interventions with individuals in work settings.

Another intervention is using **physical exercise** as a means of preventing the negative effects of stress by lowering arousal. In the first chapter of this book the stress process was said to be triggered by a 'fight or flight' response (the Alarm stage of the GAS), which includes changes in heart rate, blood flow, hormone release and muscle tension. Matteson and Ivancevich (1987) explained that the purpose of this fight–flight response is to prepare the body for action. In many stressful situations, however, action does not follow exposure to a stressor. Thus, exercise can act as a release for these physical processes. Research has consistently shown that routine vigorous activity is an effective strategy for preventing the negative effects of stress (for a review, see Ledwidge, 1980). The exact process by which physical exercise mediates the psychological state of stress is not completely understood. It has been hypothesized that just as the mind affects the body in psychosomatic illness, a 'somatopsychic' relationship exists when physical activity produces a positive psychological response (Harris, 1973).

In a review of the literature on the effects of exercise in

preventing stress, Jette (1984) concluded that three variables are important: type, frequency and duration of exercise. The type of exercise that produces the most positive effects is aerobic exercise, using large muscles to move body weight against gravity or over a distance with rhythmic or dynamic movements. Examples of aerobic exercise are jogging, cycling and swimming (Haskell, 1984). In terms of frequency, aerobic exercise is suggested three to four times per week, with some differences depending on the type of exercise used. The duration of these exercise sessions should be about 30 to 40 minutes at 50 to 60 per cent of maximal working capacity. Table 5.7 offers a description of several different kinds of exercise.

A major problem with using exercise in helping individuals deal with stress is 'adherence'. We know that it is difficult for adults to adhere to a regularly scheduled exercise programme, with many studies documenting a huge drop-off rate for pursuing regular exercise. The use of goal setting has been suggested as a means of increasing adherence (Martin and Dubbert, 1982). In addition, adherence rates increase when people are educated about the benefits of exercise and when programmes are tailored to meet individual preferences and schedules. Behavioural techniques have also been used to improve adherence: examples are cues or stimuli (for example, charts), self-monitoring (for example, maintaining an exercise log) and goal contracting.

Several of these guidelines for increasing adherence have been used by organizations in efforts to help promote exercise as a means of dealing with stress among employees. In large organizations, it has been possible to provide on-site exercise facilities. In organizations where such facilities are not feasible, practitioners might consider other options to encourage regular exercise among employees. Some companies negotiate corporate membership rates at local health clubs. In addition, practitioners might consider organizing exercise programmes that do not necessitate special facilities. At one university, the health service department organized a programme in which employees kept track of miles walked during lunch hours. Individual employees and departments that met their goals were recognized in the university newsletter. Simply publishing information about the value of various kinds of exercise can be a real service to employees. Sample materials that could be used in this way are included in Chapter 8.

Another problem with stress management interventions is that they must be carefully designed with regard to the expectations that organizations have for their implementation. Exhibit 5.1 discusses some difficulties experienced by practitioners as they attempted to deliver a programme.

Table 5.7   *Value of various exercises*

Energy range* (Approximate calories used per hour)	Activity	Benefits
72–84	Sitting conversing	Of no conditioning value.
120–50	Strolling, 1 m.p.h. Walking, 2 m.p.h.	Not sufficiently strenuous to promote endurance unless your exercise capacity is very low.
150–240	Cleaning windows Mopping floors Vacuuming	Adequate for conditioning if carried out continuously for 20–30 minutes.
	Bowling Walking, 3 m.p.h. Cycling, 6 m.p.h.	Too intermittent; not sufficiently taxing to promote endurance. Adequate dynamic exercise if your capacity is low.
	Golf, pulling cart	Useful for conditioning if you walk briskly, but if cart is heavy, isometrics may be involved.
300–60	Scrubbing floors Walking, 3.5 m.p.h. Cycling, 8 m.p.h.	Adequate endurance exercise if carried out in at least 2 minute stints. Usually good dynamic aerobic exercise.
	Table tennis Badminton Volleyball	Vigorous continuous play can have endurance benefits. Otherwise, only promotes skill.
	Golf, carrying clubs	Promotes endurance if you reach and maintain target heart rate. Aids strength and skill.
	Tennis, doubles	Not very beneficial unless there is continuous play for at least 2 minutes at a time. Aids skill.
	Many calisthenics Ballet exercises	Will promote endurance if continuous, rhythmic and repetitive. Promotes agility, coordination and muscle strength. Those requiring isometric effort, such as push-ups and sit-ups, not good for cardio-vascular fitness.
360–420	Walking, 4 m.p.h. Cycling, 10 m.p.h. Ice or roller skating	Dynamic, aerobic and beneficial. Skating should be done continuously.
420–80	Walking, 5 m.p.h. Cycling, 11 m.p.h. Tennis, singles	Dynamic, aerobic and beneficial. Can provide benefit if played 30 minutes or more with an attempt to keep moving.
	Water skiing	Total isometrics. Very risky for person with high risk of heart disease or deconditioned normals.
480–600	Jogging, 5 m.p.h. Cycling, 12 m.p.h.	Dynamic, aerobic, endurance-building exercise.
	Downhill skiing	Runs are usually too short to promote ·endurance significantly. Mostly benefits skill. Combined stress of altitude, cold

Table 5.7 *cont.*

Energy range* (Approximate calories used per hour)	Activity	Benefits
		and exercise may be too great for some heart patients.
	Paddleball	Not sufficiently continuous. Promotes skill.
600–60	Running, 5.5 m.p.h. Cycling, 13 m.p.h.	Excellent conditioner.
Above 600	Running, 6 or more m.p.h.	Excellent conditioner.
	Handball Squash	Competitive environment in hot room is dangerous to anyone not in excellent physical condition. Can provide conditioning benefits if played 30 minutes or more with attempt to keep moving.
	Swimming†	Good conditioning exercise – if continuous strokes. Especially good for persons who can't tolerate weight-bearing exercise, such as those with joint disease.

*   In all activities, energy used will vary depending on skill, rest patterns, environmental temperature and body size.
†   Wide calorie range depending on skill of swimmer, stroke, temperature of water, body composition, current and other factors.

Exhibit 5.1

Stress Management Intervention

Lois Campolo and Tom Padgett

A local business contacted Briar Cliff College for help with corporate training of its employees. The company had recently undergone phenomenal growth, from a handful of employees to well over 1,500. Due to such rapid growth many core employees were being passed over for management positions by newly recruited people with advanced training and experience.

Since the college has been historically supportive of cooperative efforts between faculty and administrators, Briar Cliff's Center for Professional Development asked us to develop an eight hour stress management curriculum. It was envisioned that the curriculum would be delivered to hundreds, if not all, of the employees. We codeveloped the course to be delivered by each presenter in identical format.

The company was very anxious to get the training programme off the ground and in essence wanted everything to start 'yesterday'. Consequently, Briar Cliff put a great deal of pressure on us to be 'up and running' with our programme within days. Our first problem was to convince both the college and the company that we needed more time to custom fit our programme to the unique needs of the employees. As 'stress management' can be defined in so many ways by different clients, we first met with a human resource management person. After that, we requested a meeting with a cross-section of employees to better understand their definition of stress. We spent the better part of two hours with this employee group whose members demonstrated their need for stress management.

We highly recommend 'custom fitting' a programme to meet the needs of clients as it personalizes the programme and gives you a chance to gain knowledge of the personality of the organization. In this particular case, we learned that the extremely high level of corporate stress was due to a rapidly changing corporate structure, incredible company growth and a great deal of employee role ambiguity. A number of more senior employees had seen their decision making capabilities greatly reduced. These same employees had been the ones responsible for the tremendous success of the company and, thus, their frustration level was very high.

It was decided that a practical 'hands on' interactive workshop format would be most conducive to meeting the diverse employee needs. Delivery consisted of two, four-hour workshops held on company time during two consecutive weeks. The focus was on learning to identify lifestyle and job related sources of stress, to identify effective attitudes and approaches for managing stress, and to facilitate the development of positive habits and skills that help individuals to be productive and reach personal targets.

Unfortunately, we each delivered only one complete eight-hour workshop serving no more than about 20 of the intended 1,000 employees. One of the major pitfalls was the intermediary position the college played between ourselves and the business. Colleges and universities can be good sources of contact. However, once the contact had been established, it would have been better for us to maintain autonomy and work directly with the business or agency with whom we were consulting. In this way, we would maintain control over communication and could set specific parameters with the client.

In addition to the confusion of using a 'middleman', the frenetic nature of the company doomed the project. Inaccurate memos with regard to time and place of workshop were sent from the company to the employees. The company's lack of clarity about the project's goals resulted in anger and confusion on the part of employees which in turn cut down on anticipated workshop attendance and participation. Due to time constraints, we were unable to negotiate for workshop facilities that allowed the interactive nature of our workshop format. Our facilities were not physically conducive to the relaxation exercises we had planned.

At the end of our initial set of stress management programmes, the company evaluated the sessions using a standard corporate form that did not relate to the specific format or nature of our workshop. We suggest you work with the client to develop an evaluation form that provides worthwhile information to both you and the client.

When doing corporate stress management, ironically, the company that is most needy is also likely to be least capable of providing the leadership necessary to structure the consultation at the corporate level. When all was said and done, we had a project to deliver but no one to deliver it to. The project died after one delivery.

In summary, the six key elements of our experience are:

1 After initial contact, always deal directly with the client, not through a middleman.
2 Custom fit the programme to your client's needs.
3 Communicate clearly with the client so that you both understand the goals of the programme.
4 Negotiate facilities that will be most conducive to delivery of your training programme.
5 Maintain control over evaluation.
6 Don't be discouraged if the client that could most use your help chooses not to.

Lois Campolo is Coordinator of Counseling Services at Briar Cliff College in Sioux City, Iowa. She is currently involved in Critical Incident Stress Debriefing of emergency responders in Northwest Iowa.

Tom Padgett is Professor and Chairperson of the Department of Psychology at Briar Cliff College. He previously served as Vice President of Student Development at the college.

All of the techniques described in this chapter so far have been primarily aimed at preventing the negative effects of stress. In the introduction to this chapter we said that other types of coping strategies are combative in nature; that is they are designed to combat the effects of stress that are unavoidable. The remaining techniques described in this chapter represent combative coping strategies.

Combative Strategies

Developing Coping Resources

In reviewing Table 5.1, you will see that there are three classes of intervention associated with combative coping strategies. The first of these classes focuses on developing coping resources. Several of the intervention techniques in the previous section on preventive strategies might also serve as coping resources. In the introduction to this chapter, we used the example of assertiveness training; in some situations assertiveness skills might be viewed as preventive, while actually using the skills for a problem already existing might better be labelled combative. Other skills discussed in the first half of this chapter that can be combative when used to deal with inevitable stress are problem solving, social skills, negotiation skills and relaxation. Several additional coping skills are primarily associated with combating stress that is unavoidable.

Research evidence suggests that **social support** is effective in combating stress (Wells, 1984). As we discussed in Chapter 2, social support is effective in reducing occupational stress because of the 'triple threat' it poses. More specifically, social support affects occupational stress in three ways. Two of these ways are 'main effects': first, social support can directly enhance health by meeting human needs for affection, appreciation, social contact and security; and secondly, social support can reduce interpersonal tension in a work environment and thus directly affect the levels of stress. The other way in which social support is effective in combating occupational stress is a buffering or interactive effect. Social support modifies the relationship between stress and health and protects an individual from the negative effects of stress. Besides helping the individual cope with stress, social support is associated with improvements in other areas of organizational functioning (for example, participation and satisfaction) (Beehr, 1985b). The ways in which organizations might benefit from social support will be discussed in the next chapter.

One other coping resource strategy is worth noting. **Time management** has been identified as a useful resource in helping workers develop coping responses. The popular press is full of information about how to manage time effectively. Similarly, practitioners have concerned themselves with developing ways to help people combat stress through effective time management. These strategies are often focused on two areas – knowledge acquisition and skill development – and are delivered in the form of training programmes.

Several authors have suggested information that can be useful in developing time management programmes (see Bonoma and Slevin, 1978; Steward, 1978). One important area to consider is the extent to which an individual has adequate knowledge of job responsibilities, duties and authority, since lacking this knowledge can lead a worker to waste time doing tasks that are not central to a specific job. One way to intervene is to have employees work with supervisors to clarify expectations associated with specific jobs and to identify parts of work where the employee has authority to act alone or enlist the support of others. Another aspect to consider in developing time management interventions is how much employees know about how they allocate time among different duties at work. One effective technique is to have employees keep a log of the time they spend on specific duties for a period of several weeks. Analyses of these logs can help the worker determine if actual allocation of time matches the duties and responsibilities of the job.

In addition to increasing understanding about allocation of time, time management interventions should include education and skill development in prioritization. The Pareto principle has been used to describe a situation that often occurs in the workplace when priorities are not clear. This principle suggests that 80 per cent of time at work is spent on duties that are related to 20 per cent of important job outcomes. Thus without prioritizing, an employee might spend 80 per cent of work time on duties that do not lead to important results (for example, doing tasks that are quick and easy to accomplish). Effective time management training should include instruction and exercises that encourage workers to outline and prioritize duties of their jobs. Table 5.8 offers a sample exercise that employees might complete to help clarify some of the suggestions outlined in this section.

In addition to priorities at work, individuals have needs and

Table 5.8   *Clarification of job functions*

Now that you have checked the responsibilities which make up important elements of your job, review the list and group similar or related responsibilities together. These groupings constitute job functions. For example, you might feel that contacting customers, maintaining contacts and responding to customer needs are related responsibilities which would constitute a function called 'customer relations'. Training personnel, selecting and hiring staff and delegating work assignments might be grouped into a job function called 'staffing'. You can title your job functions by any descriptive name you wish.

Normally, a position consists of from five to eight important functions, including a 'miscellaneous' function. Miscellaneous may be made up of a number of less important responsibilities.

Directions

Please group the responsibilities on your check list into not less than five or more than eight functions and list them in the following table.

1   Name each function.
2   List those specific responsibilities which define the function.
3   Estimate the overall value or importance of each functional area to the organization. (This should total 100 per cent including miscellaneous.) It may not always correspond to the amount of time spent in the function.
4   After this has been accomplished, discuss the results with your supervisor.

Name of function	Specific responsibilities	Rated importance	Percentage of time

aspirations outside of work and beyond their current positions. Including goal setting instructions in a time management programme can help an employee identify important career goals and life values. This instruction might include exercises that allow employees to write a 'mission statement' about the things in life and work they value most. In turn, they can develop specific goals to help them reach their missions as well as action steps to follow in pursuing their goals.

After participating in a goal setting workshop, one employee developed the following mission and goals:

Mission: At this point in my career, I would like to focus on continuing to expand my skills as I learn more about this organization and my profession. At the same time, I would like to continue to work at maintaining a healthy balance between work and life outside of work.

Goals:
1 Talk with my supervisor in my next performance review about becoming involved in one new project in the coming year that will give me broader exposure to the entire organization.
2 Join a professional association and attend one meeting each quarter.
3 Sign up for a couples golf league for spring and summer that will allow me to enjoy playing more regularly and to spend time in an activity that my spouse and I both enjoy.

Finally, time management interventions should focus on helping employees identify 'time robbers' (such as, meetings, visitors, inaccessible records, trouble shooting, paper work, returning phone calls). Employees should be encouraged to develop specific strategies to conserve time (for example, speed reading, using form letters), to control time (for example, more realistic scheduling, awareness of cyclical crunches such as quarterly reports) and to make time (for example, effective delegation to subordinates, more effective advance planning).

In this section, we have discussed two coping resources that are important in helping individuals combat the negative effects of stress. The next section covers the second class of combative coping strategies: altering stress-inducing behaviour patterns.

Altering Stress-Inducing Behaviour Patterns
In previous chapters, we described factors unique to the individual related to stress. It was suggested that certain individual characteristics are associated with increased negative consequences resulting from stress. Thus, a target of intervention in helping individuals combat stress is the alteration of behaviour patterns known to be stress-inducing. One useful construct in understanding this intervention strategy is the **Type A Behaviour Pattern** described in detail in Chapter 3. The behaviours that are characteristic of individuals who are diagnosed as being Type A leave them at obvious risk for negative stress reactions (for example, competitive, hard driving, intense, high need for control, sense of time urgency, impatience, aggressiveness, hostility).

Treatment of individuals exhibiting these behaviour patterns has been the subject of a great deal of research (for a review, see Roskies, 1987). Despite the number of research studies, specific findings which lead to treatment have not been conclusive. Several factors account for the difficulty in developing effective treatment interventions with Type A individuals. First, while there is clear evidence that Type A individuals are at risk from heart disease, it is not clear what aspect of their behavioural, psychological, or emotional functioning makes them vulnerable. Thus, there is no clear direction for an intervention. In addition, treatment is difficult because of a motivation factor. More specifically, there is some question as to whether Type A individuals see a need to change; similarly, there is some question as to whether managers are motivated to see Type A individuals change. Given organizational climate and societal norms that value aspects of the Type A behaviour pattern, there may be reluctance on the part of some managers to see Type A individuals change completely (Matteson and Ivancevich, 1987).

Despite these difficulties, efforts have been undertaken to implement stress management for Type A individuals. For instance, Suinn (1982) developed a modification programme for post-heart attack patients. This programme included training in muscle relaxation, identifying varying degrees of muscle tension, relaxing as a coping response to stressful situations and using imagery to practise behaviour incompatible with Type A behaviour. When compared with a control group who did not receive treatment, patients in the training programme reported more lifestyle changes and greater improvement in subjective and physiological responses to stress. Another example of a treatment programme for Type A behaviour has been developed at the Recurrent Coronary Prevention Project (RCPP). This programme includes a series of drills that are used with Type A individuals, such as playing to lose in sports and recreation, developing a log of things that lead to anger, and beginning to laugh at oneself (Powell, 1984). Perhaps the most extensive treatment programme for Type A behaviour is described by Roskies (1987) in her book *Stress Management for the Healthy Type A*. The programme is divided into eight modules listed in Table 5.9 and is designed for use with 'healthy' Type A individuals such as managers and professionals.

These programmes and the other techniques described throughout the chapter might be useful in helping individuals alter stress-inducing behaviour patterns. These interventions are particularly important given the severe health risks associated with these behaviour patterns. The practitioner might encourage management support for intervention efforts by comparing the costs of these treatment programmes with the potential health costs that might result if the programmes are not implemented.

Avoiding Stressors Through Life Adjustment and Adjusting Demand Levels

As a final set of combative strategies, we turn to a discussion of interventions that help individuals deal with stress through life and

Table 5.9 *Stress management programme for Type A individuals*

Modules	Skills taught
1 Introduction to the programme.	General overview.
2 *Relax*: learning to control physical stress responses.	Self-monitoring of physical and emotional tension signs, progressive muscle relaxation.
3 *Control yourself*: learning to control behavioural stress responses.	Self-monitoring of behavioural signs of tension; incompatible behaviours, delay, communication skills.
4 *Think productively*: learning to control cognitive stress responses.	Self-monitoring of self-talk; cognitive restructuring.
5 *Be prepared*: learning to anticipate and plan for predictable stress situations.	Identification of recurrent stress triggers; stress inoculation training.
6 *Cool it*: learning emergency braking in unpredictable stress situations.	Identification of signs of heightened tension; application of physical, behavioural and cognitive controls; anger control.
7 *Building stress resistance*: learning to plan for rest and recuperation.	Identification of pleasurable activities; problem solving.
8 *Protecting your investment*: stress management as a lifelong investment.	Relapse prevention.

work adjustment. As an introductory note, many of the methods for making these kinds of adjustments will be covered in the next chapter on workplace interventions. Two special combative interventions, dealing with work, marriage and family, and career concerns are included here because of the importance these areas hold for the individual.

Some of the factors identified in Chapter 3 as having important implications for occupational stress management involved the changing demographics of the workforce: working women, working parents, single parents and dual career couples. Because of the potential stress that individuals encounter in relation to these variables, they represent important areas of concern for the practitioner. Organizations are only beginning to respond to the needs of the changing workforce. In the meantime, it is the role of a human service practitioner to help individuals cope with the stress they encounter when their work and personal lives conflict.

One possible intervention strategy is to offer guidance and training to individuals who attempt to balance the demands of work and home life. The skills that have been outlined throughout this chapter might be tailored to fit the needs of these employees. For instance, effective communication skills will be useful for dual career couples who cope with two partners' careers. Similarly, negotiation and assertiveness training might benefit the parent who is trying to propose an alternative work schedule to her supervisor to accommodate child-care needs. In addition, time management skills might help an employee cope with the demands of work and home associated with being a single parent. Finally, creative problem solving could help manage stress experienced by a work group when they are forced to 'cover' the duties of a co-worker who is working less because of parental leave.

Several authors have begun to write about ways to cope with the competing demands and stressors of family and work life. One notable example is a book by Dynerman and Hayes (1991). These researchers interviewed several hundred people and, based on the these interviews, compiled a series of examples of the ways people have made adjustments in their work and home lives to combat the effects of stress. In addition, the book contains a number of practical suggestions for planning for these stressors, negotiating flexible work options, and dealing with jobs after a creative work schedule or situation has been developed.

As with other suggestions outlined in this chapter, a practitioner will need to be creative in devising ways to teach employees with special work needs about skills that will help them manage stress. Some of the suggestions outlined above represent a good match for making pertinent information available: articles in newsletters, speaker series and video/audiotapes. In addition, practitioners have begun holding support groups in some organizations. Examples of these groups include working parent groups, single parent groups and groups for employees who have returned to college. As another creative intervention, a practitioner has organized a series of panels to discuss dealing with work/life demands. This practitioner uses employees from the corporation as speakers for these panels. Feedback on this programme indicates that hearing their co-workers speak makes some of the demands seem more manageable because fellow employees know their company better than any outside 'expert' ever would. As a final example, one organization has developed a working parent resource centre that contains a variety of information of interest to parents including a clearinghouse of day care resources.

Beyond the stress experienced in balancing work and home life, every worker must combat the stress that arises from concern about careers. In Chapter 4 we outlined specific stressors associated with different **career stages**. As noted in this discussion,

Table 5.10 *Model of organizational career development*

Career planning	Career management
(individual)	(organization)
examples of activities:	*examples of activities:*
Self-assessment	Selection/hiring
Choice of career field	Job rotation
Choice of job assignments	Promotion
Choice of organization/company	Performance appraisal
Monitoring career opportunities	Training
Preparation of career strategy/plan	Continuing education/reimbursement
Implementation of plan	

a number of these stressors are the result of the human resource management practices pursued by an organization. The practitioner can, however, help individuals combat these stressors using interventions that are aimed at the development of coping strategies within the control of the individual.

One useful model in understanding these interventions is presented by Hall (1986). This model (depicted in Table 5.10) explains organizational career development as being comprised of two components: career planning and career management. The difference in these two components of career development within organizations is the responsibility assumed for activities in each area. **Career management** is the responsibility of the organization and includes activities such as recruitment, selection, promotion, training and succession planning. **Career planning**, on the other hand, is the responsibility of the individual and involves activities of job choice; choice of organization; assessment of skills, interests, and values; and monitoring career opportunities. A practitioner can help combat stress by focusing individuals on those career activities within their control. Through seminars, testing, resource materials and individual counselling, a practitioner can assist the worker from moving beyond being passive about career and life planning to taking a more active role in these activities.

Consider the practitioner who is working with Bob, a PhD level scientist at a major manufacturing company. Bob was recruited to the company because his research interests were a match for a new area of research and development that the company was pursuing. Since he arrived at the company, economic conditions have changed and the organization is no longer pursuing the development of the product in his area of expertise. So, Bob has been shuffled between small projects that are not a match for his skills or interests. Because he has little work to do, he has become bored at work and his performance has deteriorated. Bob might come to a practitioner complaining about 'the company' and how 'they' have ruined his career. Acknowledging the frustration that he is feeling, the practitioner might help Bob by sharing the organizational career development model and the activities of career planning that Bob might pursue. For instance, he might spend his free time networking with people in other departments to see if there is a better match for his skills in some other area of the company. Bob might also consider continuing education as a way of developing skills to make him more versatile in pursuing other job opportunities. Finally, Bob might opt to look for a position outside of the company in an organization that is a better match for his skills. In fact, Bob might look at his situation as an opportunity to pursue teaching or consulting, career interests that have not been fulfilled in his current laboratory work. No matter which option he chooses, the practitioner has offered realistic options to help Bob combat the stress of his current career situation.

In reviewing the strategies presented in this chapter, it is apparent that there are many ways to help individuals combat and even prevent the stress encountered in relation to work. However, it is clear that even though a practitioner might intervene with an individual to deal with stress, the reality of the workplace may not be changed. Dealing with stress associated with the workplace is the topic covered in the next chapter. Interventions aimed at changing the workplace are outlined along with suggestions about how a practitioner can help to bring about these changes.

6
Workplace Interventions

An increasing number of organizations are developing programmes that focus on occupational stress. In fact, in 1988 about 26 per cent of the organizations in the United States reported having at least one stress management programme, with another 25 per cent of organizations saying plans for developing a programme were underway (Murphy, 1984). Despite the prevalence of stress management programmes, some concern has been expressed about whether the kinds of interventions sponsored by organizations can be or will be effective in helping workers deal with stress.

Many of the stress management programmes currently in place in organizations have been described as mere 'band aids' for the real problem of stress (Murphy, 1984). More specifically, intervention strategies in current stress management programmes seem to fall short in several ways. First, programmes offered in many organizations are 'curative' in nature. Thus, the strategies introduced in work sites are aimed at curing problems after workers experience the negative effects of stress. As seen in the medical field in recent years, a better approach to managing stress would include interventions that are 'preventive'. In this way, intervention programmes would not be designed with stress conceptualized as a disease that must be cured after its symptoms are already causing difficulty (Ivancevich and Matteson, 1980). Instead, such approaches would intervene before an individual actually experiences stress.

Another problem with current stress management programmes in organizations is the way they are designed to meet the needs of different employee groups. In Chapter 4, there was a brief discussion of differences in factors that white and blue collar workers perceive as stressful. In particular, there are different environments in which these two groups of employees work and different kinds of job tasks that they do. Results from a telephone survey conducted in the United States by the National Institute for Occupational Safety and Health (NIOSH) identified significant differences in the stress factors identified for corporate vs. labour groups (Neale et al., 1983). The study showed that leaders from these two groups demonstrated a 'selective attention' with regard to the kinds of stress factors that they believe are operating in the work environment. Given these biases, it would seem logical that the same sort of bias could occur in the design of organizational stress interventions.

As a final comment on the occasional ineffectiveness of stress management programmes, consider the target of intervention which is often primarily focused on the individual. While intervention with the individual represents an important component in an overall effort to deal with stress in the workplace, this approach does not represent a complete intervention strategy. To deal effectively with stress as it is experienced by employees, management and practitioners within organizations must consider ways in which the work environment might be contributing to the problem. In particular, they might consider changes that could be made in the organization either to alleviate stressful situations for individuals or to help them cope with stress when it is encountered. By simply intervening with the individual, a 'blame the victim' situation is created: employees who are the victims of stressful working conditions are blamed for the stress they are experiencing. A better approach might be a strategy in which *both* the individual and the organization are targets for intervention. Thus, the techniques described in the previous chapter represent a supplement to changes in the work environment and the organization. Workplace intervention strategies are the focus of this chapter.

A number of different methods have been suggested to alter the workplace in order to help individuals deal with stress. Similarly, several different ways of grouping or categorizing these intervention methods have been offered. In a review of how the field of psychology is responding to occupational stress, Sauter *et al.* (1990) suggested that interventions be grouped into four distinct categories: first, job design to improve working conditions; secondly, surveillance of psychological disorders and risk factors; thirdly, information dissemination and training; and fourthly, enrichment of psychological health services for workers. While these categories represent a good framework for conceptualizing how the mental health field might deal with occupational stress, they are too broad for the practitioner who is working in a single organization. Instead, the interventions presented in this chapter will be categorized according to the framework of workplace stress factors that were discussed in Chapter 4. The categories included: role characteristics; job characteristics; interpersonal relationships; organizational structure and climate; and human resource management systems. These categories were identified as key intervention points a practitioner might consider in planning interventions.

Role Characteristics

As noted in previous chapters, the study of psycho-social stressors in relation to occupational stress began with the consideration of role characteristics. A number of different role characteristics have been linked to the occurrence of occupational stress. Similarly, various techniques have been proposed for dealing with the difficulty that role characteristics might cause. For instance, situations in which workers have a well defined sense of their job responsibilities lead to a decrease in the amount of role ambiguity encountered (Sauter *et al.*, 1990). This understanding of job responsibility can be fostered by managers and supervisors if they work with employees to ensure that duties are clearly defined and tasks are understood. Thus, managers should consider how they communicate with their employees about the core requirements of a job. In particular, the supervisor should avoid simply using **job descriptions** that outline the duties an employee will be asked to perform and instead help employees to focus on job functions.

You might recall that in Chapter 5, an exercise for outlining job functions was presented (see Table 5.8). Using this exercise a counsellor, for example, could move beyond a simple list of job **duties** and develop clusters of duties that form **functions** of his job:

Priority	*Name of function*	*Specific responsibilities*
1	Individual counselling	Conducting 25 individual sessions per week.
		Serving as emergency/walk-in counsellor one afternoon per week.
2	Group counselling	Facilitating one therapy group each week.
		Facilitating one support group each week.
5	Outreach programming	Offering two community-wide programmes each month.
		Consulting with community groups about mental health issues.
4	Administration	Attending agency staff meeting each week.
		Maintaining client records.
		Completing agency and insurance forms.

Priority	Name of function	Specific responsibilities
3	Professional development	Attending case consultation conference each week.
		Attending professional association meeting each month.
		Attending national conference once each year.
		Reading journals and new books.

After the counsellor developed this list of functions and responsibilities, he could discuss it with his supervisor. If discrepancy existed between how the counsellor and the supervisor ranked the importance of each function or the amount of time to be allocated to each of the responsibilities, some negotiation and clarification could occur. This clarification could in turn lead to decrease role confusion for the counsellor.

In order to be most effective in alleviating role ambiguity and confusion, any description of a job should be behaviour-based. As an example, a manager could increase the clarity of an employee's job responsibilities by avoiding phrases such as 'creative' or 'cooperative' and instead use descriptions such as the following:

Creative:
John consistently serves as a creative force on our work team. In particular, he has offered solutions to four major production problems we have encountered in the last year. One of these solutions resulted in a cost savings of £300,000 for our company.

Cooperative:
John is a very cooperative employee. He offers to answer telephones on the two afternoons per month when our secretary is involved in completing payroll.

Ivancevich and Matteson (1980) described a method for combating role ambiguity and role conflict that involves both the supervisor and the employee. This technique is labelled **role analysis and clarification** and is based on the premise that the best source of information about a job can be provided by the person in the job (the role occupant). Role analysis and clarification involves getting the individual in the job to answer several questions that are then discussed by the role occupant and the supervisor. These questions might include: What do you think is expected of you in this job?; What do you expect of me as your supervisor?; What sort of information/resources do you need to do the job well?; What areas of trouble/difficulty do you anticipate as you begin the job? Based on these questions, both the manager and the employee can move to an increased understanding of the perception held by the other. If there are discrepancies in the expectations of either party, they can be discussed before they arise as problems in performance.

As an example, return to the case of the counsellor outlined above (see p. 91) where the following conversation might take place:

> *Supervisor*: Well I've reviewed the job functions and responsibilities that you've developed and I think you've described your job very well. I suppose I'm concerned about the priority that you've attached to each of the functions.
>
> *Counsellor*: What do you mean?
>
> *Supervisor*: Well I see you've assigned the lowest priority (5) to outreach programming.
>
> *Counsellor*: Is that a problem?
>
> *Supervisor*: Yes, it could be. I am getting pressure from our board of directors to be more visible and active in the community. In addition, the mental health field is moving more towards a proactive approach to delivering services to groups beyond traditional counselling approaches.
>
> *Counsellor*: I suppose I ranked the job functions as I see them in my job.
>
> *Supervisor*: And I want you to know I appreciate your input – you know the job because you do it. Let's see if we can estimate how much time each of these activities takes in a given month and then see what sort of compromise we can reach.

Thus the supervisor and employee would be able to reach agreement before the counsellor began doing his job. The desired outcome of this discussion would be to reduce potential role difficulty and subsequent confusion and stress for both the counsellor and the supervisor. In organizations where job duties are outlined in this way, stress can be reduced as employees and supervisors operate with common understanding about the work that needs to be done.

Several other role characteristics associated with job stress are role overload and role underload. To deal with stress associated with these role characteristics, it is first important that the manager or supervisor understand the job and the actual work required within the role. Managers must move beyond simply conceptualizing role overload or underload as being associated with work pace or the amount of work required and instead consider more subtle factors that can affect overload or underload such as the amount of person contact required or the number of decisions that are made independently. Besides simply understanding what factors are affecting workers, the manager should also consider the extent to which workers believe they can discuss the perceptions or feelings they have of being overloaded or underloaded. Managers might strive to create an environment in which workers feel safe to present concerns they have about too much or too little to do. Such an environment would not only include an openness to dealing with stress but would also reflect a standing operating procedure (SOP) which would allow workers to say no to excessive demands and to work collaboratively to develop solutions when they do experience stress.

For example consider this description of a supervisor offered by Juan who works in a small office:

> I can't tell you how much it has helped to have Greg as our manager. It feels like a new place – he has changed things so I don't feel stressed out all the time. He doesn't bite our heads off if we say there is a problem. In the past, if you even mentioned you were having a problem or falling behind you'd be in trouble. Our old boss would start watching you more carefully and say if we didn't like it you could find another job. Greg is willing to hear our concerns. He listens patiently and then tries to figure out a way to help us deal with the problem. People feel much more free and are even willing to help come up with solutions to problems of other people on the staff.

As a final note on role characteristics, consider the importance of individual differences. In Chapter 3, we suggested that there are a number of individual difference variables that affect the way in which various individuals will perceive, react and cope with stress. This observation is especially important in implementing any of the suggestions that have been offered in this section. More specifically, the manager should recognize that the role characteristics which will result in stress for one worker will not necessarily be the same for another. Thus, no single formula exists for prescribing the best possible way to deal with stress in relation to role characteristics. What can be generalized across the suggestions offered here is a real need for managers and their subordinates to have open and clear discussions about work roles and expectations. This open communication, along with the recognition and appreciation of individual differences, will leave the manager and employee ready to utilize some of the job design methods discussed in the next section.

As a way of understanding how role characteristics can help a manager deal with different employees, consider Steve who serves as director of a small agency employing about 10 people. In conducting end-of-year progress reports, Steve draws these conclusions about two of his employees:

> Marie is in her first year of employment with the agency. Because she is new to the agency and the profession, she has a lot of energy and

enthusiasm for her work, especially taking on increased responsibility. Steve concludes that it will be most helpful to assist Marie set realistic goals about which project she might begin in the next three months. By helping her set these goals, Marie will feel assured she can increase responsibility and gain new experiences while Steve can feel more assured as manager that Marie will not overextend herself and suffer burnout.

Betty is beginning her seventh year with the agency. She has had success with every project she has been assigned. She has been the top performer in the agency for the last five years in a row. Because she has been around for a long time, a number of the agency's customers and clients have come to know and respect Betty. In fact as she prepared for maternity leave after the birth of her second child, Betty continually hears that the customers won't know what to do while she is gone. Knowing that Betty might experience unnecessary stress as a result of this subtle pressure from customers, Steve helps her to devise a way to announce her temporary leave. In addition they discuss a way that she might introduce staff members to key customers so they feel they have a personal contact in her absence.

Job Characteristics

Having discovered the nature of a potential stressor using the suggestions in the previous section, the supervisor and the worker are now confronted with the task of deciding how to respond. Practitioners who are faced with this situation directly or in consultation with a supervisor or manager should consider how to improve job characteristics. The notion of being involved in consultation with regard to job characteristics is mentioned because many human service practitioners find themselves offering consultation to managers who are attempting to help their employees deal with stress. In many work settings the management staff is comprised of individuals who do not have the kind of background or experience that prepares them to develop strategies for dealing with unhealthy or unproductive jobs. In fact, it has been suggested that one important intervention strategy might be to seek ways to train managers and engineering personnel in the area of job design.

Without having to be an expert, there are many ways that a human resource practitioner can intervene in response to job characteristics and stress. One useful tool is a model comprising four elements, or conditions, said to affect the relationship between stress and performance on a particular job: task stress, operation of other stressors, a coping process and an indicator of stress. Each of these conditions is defined in Table 6.1. Using this model, the practitioner attempting to help an individual deal with a stressful

Table 6.1   *Conditions of stress in job tasks and performance*

Conditions	Definitions/examples
1 Task stress	Stress associated with some primary task required to do the job (e.g., overload, responsibility for people, ambiguity, conflict, physical danger).
2 Operation of other stressors	Stress associated with factors not directly related to primary job tasks (e.g., poor co-worker relationships, financial worries, marital/family concerns, career issues).
3 A coping process	A behaviour that reduces the stress an individual experiences (e.g., exercising during lunch, developing a method of completing a task that reduces time, negotiating with boss to receive help on some part of a project).
4 An indicator of stress	Observation of task performance by a manager to estimate amount of stress being experienced by an employee (e.g., erratic performance by a consistently good performer, increase in time needed to complete a routine task, increase in number of errors in work).

job situation could consider *each* of the four conditions and decide about the most effective intervention.

As an example of how this model might be used, consider the case of Mary who works in a financial aid department at a university. Poor economic times and increased standards for eligibility have made it increasingly difficult for students to qualify for financial aid grants and loans. Because more and more students are coming to the office with questions and comments about their financial situation, Mary finds herself spending extra time handling walk-in calls. She has noted that even though she does not change the situation in which a student is 'stuck', often it appears to help simply to listen to the student. Because of the increased student/customer contact, Mary finds herself falling behind in processing financial aid applications (which represents a major portion of her job responsibilities). She has fallen so far behind that she missed several important deadlines that have meant several students will not be considered for loans.

Using the model described above, the manager of her department might consider several different ways to deal with the situation and offer assistance to Mary. In this case, the **task stress** is associated with falling behind on processing loan applications. The manager might anticipate that Mary is being detrimentally affected by stress by observing the **indicator of stress** (a decrease in the number of applications processed per week and the missed deadlines). Similarly, the manager might recognize that several additional factors (**operation of other stressors**) might be operating in Mary's life. For instance, she is enrolled as a part-time student in pursuit of a graduate degree. She is also married and has two children who are both under the age of six. The pressures of working full time, attending classes, keeping up with assignments, and trying to maintain her family life have left Mary feeling very stressed, so stressed that she was willing to talk with her supervisor who was usually supportive around these issues. In addition, Mary shared with her supervisor that she has come to recognize that after graduate training she sees herself pursuing a career in counselling in a college counselling centre. Thus, the position in the financial aid department is not a good match to her future interests.

To this point, the model has aided in an improved assessment of the situation. This assessment would enable the supervisor to offer several options to Mary. The discussion with Mary might begin:

'I am aware that you have missed three deadlines that have been costly for several students and that your application processing rate has dropped by 20 per cent. I am also aware that you are under tight time constraints because of your graduate classes and family commitments and that you are anxious to finish the degree and move on in your career. I am concerned about your health and ongoing job satisfaction and about the functioning of this office, and thus we need to assess which way you think we might best intervene . . .'

After considering each of the conditions, the supervisor was able to develop a series of interventions to discuss with Mary. Focusing on task stress, the manager might suggest that some changes be made in the way Mary does the task of processing loan applications. For instance, the manager and Mary could review the process that she follows in processing applications and make an analysis of points at which she could improve efficiency. Imagine that Mary and the manager discover that a significant amount of time could be saved if Mary could use a computer program to compute the final monetary analysis. Thus, Mary might utilize new technology (computer software and hardware) or new job skills (training in system use) to alleviate some of the task stress she is experiencing.

If the manager and Mary decide that the most effective means of intervening in this situation would be to focus on the other stressors in operation, several additional strategies might be suggested. For example, if Mary reports she has trouble completing her assignments for class because she is never able to get to the library during the regular business hours because she is working, the manager and Mary might consider an alternative schedule (such as, working four 10 hour days per week with one day off for work in the library). As another alternative, the manager might suggest that Mary change to part time which would allow her to finish her degree more quickly and move into a career in the counselling field sooner. Finally, another suggestion would involve changing the duties that are required in Mary's job. If she most enjoys working with students in a counselling type relationship, perhaps Mary could handle more of the walk-in appointments and give some of her loan processing duties to another member of the department.

As a final set of intervention strategies, Mary and the manager might consider the coping process. Recall that the coping process refers to any behaviour or set of behaviours that reduces the stress an individual experiences. Such behaviours for Mary might include hiring someone to help with the tasks she does not finish at home, negotiating with her boss and graduate school adviser to do a project for class that could be completed in her office, or setting aside one hour per day during which she closes her office door and does not take appointments or phone calls in order to catch up on unfinished paper work.

In reviewing the example of Mary, several important intervention strategies were highlighted. One of these strategies is **job redesign**. Stated simply, the strategy of job redesign involves changing some aspects of the tasks that are part of a particular job. Often the focus of the redesign is to improve efficiency or effectiveness in work. In Mary's case, the job redesign suggestions included using the computer and setting aside one quiet hour during the day. As might be assumed from the example, an important starting point for intervention is a complete and thorough understanding of the job. From that point, the creativity of the supervisor, the employee and/or the consultant will determine the effectiveness of the interventions that are developed.

Another set of strategies that form a subset of job redesign interventions are those involving **job enrichment**. These strategies are described as the redefinition or restructuring of a job to make it more meaningful, challenging and intrinsically rewarding (Matteson and Ivancevich, 1987). Discussions of the importance of the principles that underlie job enrichment methodology have been proposed since the 1950s, but it was not until the 1970s that the actual practice of job enrichment was employed. In the case of

Mary, an example of job enrichment might have been to let Mary handle more of the individual meetings with students in the department because they matched her interests in counselling.

Notice that Mary's involvement in increased one-to-one meetings was coupled with a decrease in the number of loan applications she was required to process. This difference suggests an important difference between job enrichment and **job enlargement** which is a strategy that adds duties or responsibilities to a job without taking any responsibilities away. In Mary's case, the practitioner might have suggested job enlargement if she had reported being bored or unchallenged in her work (role underload). Instead, Mary was experiencing role overload and role confusion, and job enrichment was the appropriate strategy.

Several practical suggestions have been offered for how job enrichment interventions can combat the effects of occupational stress. For instance, the simplest form of job enrichment is changing a worker's responsibilities so that he or she is responsible for one piece of work. An example would be a factory worker who completes all the tasks necessary to manufacture a shoe rather than simply attaching the sole as the shoe moves along the assembly line. Interestingly, research on the effects of job enrichment programmes indicate that worker stress is significantly reduced and product quality is improved (Kopleman, 1986). Quantity, however, is not affected by the introduction of job enrichment. To return to the shoe factory, it would be hypothesized that the quality of shoe would improve because workers saw the process through from start to finish but the number of shoes produced would not increase (and may even decrease).

Beyond making a worker responsible for an entire piece of work, job enrichment can involve a wide variety of strategies. The practitioner might consider both the qualitative and quantitative nature of work in job enrichment (Jackson, 1984). This consideration is especially important in difficult economic times, when employees are not always afforded the opportunity to make changes in work that are quantitative (for instance, you may not be able to reduce the number of clients you see in a human service agency). One example involved moving five day care workers from being jointly responsible for 100 children to each having charge of 20 children. Reducing the perceived workload led to an increased feeling of control for workers, and in turn, reduced stress. In addition to this quantitative change in work, a qualitative change might also be possible. Human service workers can experience stress and burnout from prolonged contact with especially difficult clients. As a suggestion, agencies might consider mixing the case loads of providers so that no one staff member is left with one particular type of client (for example, dying patients in a hospital, convicted rapists in a prison, handicapped children in a school setting, chemical abusers in an employee assistance programme).

Besides the quantitative and qualitative nature of work, a practitioner might also consider enriching jobs in terms of their **core job features**. These features include autonomy, feedback, skill variance, task identity and task significance. These terms were defined in Chapter 4 in the discussion of task attributes. In considering these job characteristics as potential dimensions along which jobs could be enriched, it is again important to recognize the significance of individual differences. The extent to which different employees will find these various task attributes rewarding will vary greatly, thus managers should be pushed to consider how they can communicate effectively with their employees.

As a final area to be considered in this discussion of job characteristics interventions, we turn to scheduling. Recall in the description of Mary's case above that the manager suggested, as one possibility, that Mary could work four 10 hour days per week. This schedule has been termed the **compressed work week**, and this form of scheduling along with other creative approaches to doing work have become more popular in many work settings. Other examples include **flextime**, in which employees are allowed to vary their work schedule within prescribed limits, and **job sharing**, in which an employee shares the responsibilities of one full-time job with another employee.

Some research has been conducted on the use of these various scheduling variations. One study examined company records to see if schedule flexibility or an opportunity to discretionary time affected stress. Those workers who reported the greatest amount of flexibility and discretion in their schedule also reported decreased absenteeism, better work performance, greater organizational commitment and fewer psychological stress symptoms. These effects seem to be related to the amount of control a worker feels is available when scheduling is flexible (Pierce and Newstrom, 1983). In addition, these programmes are effective because they allow workers to fulfil the obligations and duties that they have outside of work (Schuler and Sethi, 1984).

Interpersonal Relationships

The importance of relationships at work has already been discussed in terms of social support (Chapter 3) and as a potential source of occupational stress in the workplace (Chapter 4). Thus, one other point of intervention is the relationships that exist among members of a work group. In considering ways to intervene, it is important to keep in mind that the relationships that exist between co-workers are characterized by different kinds of communication. In particular, communication between fellow workers might function to provide emotional support or to offer actual help in completing some job (Sauter *et al.*, 1990). Thus, the manager who is seeking to build positive relationships between workers and, in turn, decrease stress should seek ways to ensure that both kinds of communication can occur. For instance the manager might hold regular staff meetings in which employees could talk about frustrations at work and outside of work (emotional support) and about specific work-related problems and issues.

Still another way in which relationships serve as an intervention point in managing work stress is social support. As outlined in Chapter 3, there are a number of different sources of social support in the work environment. In helping an individual deal with stress at work, it is important to recognize that social support is a multi-dimensional concept. Therefore, merely focusing on the amount of support an employee feels is offered by a supervisor or boss is not enough. While support from a supervisor is a very important source of social support in buffering the effects of stress, the practitioner attempting to help employees deal with job stress should also consider the kind of support offered by co-workers, mentors, clients and subordinates (Wells, 1984).

Given the importance of the relationship with one's supervisor, the final strategy to be discussed here is targeted at the manager. As noted throughout this section, an important component in the relationships that occur at work is the communication that occurs. The more managers and supervisors can communicate effectively with workers, the less likely the worker will be to experience stress. Some particular behaviours or styles are associated with effective manager communication: achievement, contingent approval, directive, supportive, ego deflation, contingent disapproval and participative. Each of these communication behaviours is defined and illustrated in Table 6.2.

Helping managers to build skills in these communication behaviours is an important intervention strategy (Schuler and Sethi, 1984). Some practitioners have developed training programmes that teach managers and supervisors about these skills. It is surprising that even though many supervisors believe they cannot learn any new information about how to communicate, the

Table 6.2 ' *Communication behaviours for managers*

Communication behaviours	Definitions/examples
Achievement	Conveys statement of goals, challenge, confidence and high expectations. ('I am sure you can do this job even though you are new in this department.') Aids employee in knowing what is expected.
Contingent approval	Manager communicates contingent approval by praising good employee performance. ('You've done a great job on this project.')
Directive	Offers direction or guidance when the employee wants it or when the circumstances warrant it. ('Here is what you need to do today . . . and here's how I want you to do it.')
Supportive	Indicates concern for the employee as a person and not as an instrument of production. (Verbal: 'Good morning, how was your weekend?' Non-verbal: Following up on commitments, being on time.)
Ego deflation	Reverse of achievement communication behaviour. Reduces the employee's feelings of self-worth and self-confidence and makes the employee feel incapable. (Verbal: 'I can never trust you to do it right.' Non-verbal: Checking up on employees excessively.)
Contingent disapproval	Lets employee know which behaviours will be punished or not rewarded. Effective only if direction for future behaviour is included. ('You've really messed up this project. Next time have a co-worker review your plan before you start.')
Participative	Helps employee establish future goals and direction on how to best do a job. Reduces potential conflict between supervisor and employee ('How do you feel about this new assignment? Can you think of any areas in which you might have difficulty with this task?')

most basic communication skills are often new to them. Sometimes these skills can be presented in the context of other topics: conducting performance reviews, helping with employee career development, coaching performance, or facilitating meetings.

Organizational Structure and Climate

The structure and climate of a work setting also influence occupational stress experienced by an employee. At least three different intervention strategies have been suggested for dealing with stress due to climate and structure: decentralization, participative decision making and climate surveys. Each of these strategies is discussed below.

Decentralization

As noted in Chapter 4, one important concept in understanding the structure of an organization is centralization. Those organizations described as centralized (tall organizations) often have increased stress among workers. Strategies for helping promote decentralization within organizations have become increasingly popular in recent years. In particular, the attention devoted to studying Japanese organizations and management styles along with increasing use of principles associated with total quality management (TQM), as developed by Deming, have suggested methods for how organizations might decentralize. Such techniques involve changing communication patterns and networks within organizations and developing work groups (Schuler and Sethi, 1984). These groups form a team that is identified as 'autonomous' because the members determine the direction the group will follow along with the procedures and policies that will guide group members. In addition, the group also shares in rewards, with all members of the team receiving the same rewards.

In one study of semi-autonomous work groups, a department was identified as having low morale, poor work motivation and poor work attitudes. This department was allowed to function as a semi-autonomous work group; in particular, the team had control of the pace of work they did, the organization of rest breaks, and the allocations of work assignments and overtime. The supervisor no longer functioned as a leader and instead filled a support function during work times. The intervention resulted in increased feelings of autonomy, better task identity development and less emotional distress among the workers (Wall and Clegg, 1981).

Despite the success of the intervention in this study, many criticisms have been proposed about the principles of total quality management and the Japanese management style. In particular, these approaches have been labelled a 'simple fad' that will pass away like many other organizational development trends in recent decades. In addition, these strategies have been described as too simplistic for a real organization. Many people, for instance, have difficulty imagining any organization without some form of leadership. Finally, efforts in this area have been criticized because they ignore the importance of individual differences. In particular, critics claim that these strategies do not account for the great differences that exist among individuals with regard to motivation and achievement orientation. For instance, being rewarded on the basis of the performance of the team and not on individual performance may be difficult for some individuals. There does not appear to be a clear cut answer as to whether semi-autonomous work groups and similar strategies will be viable options for designing and operating organizations or whether these strategies will be helpful in attempting to alleviate problems of occupational stress.

Participative Decision Making

Another technique that is related to decentralization is **participative decision making** (PDM). PDM involves creating systems and communication channels within organizations so that employees beyond the top level of management are involved in making important decisions. By involving employees in the process of decision making, more information becomes available to them and they in turn feel a greater sense of influence and control, thus decreasing ambiguity and distress. In addition, finding ways in which workers can influence the job demands decreases the likelihood that they will experience role conflict (Murphy, 1984). PDM is characterized by two different forms within organizations: formal and informal. **Formal PDM** systems are organized and structured like unions or councils while **informal PDM** systems offer employees influence in a less structured way, such as giving input at a staff meeting (Jackson, 1984).

As one example of the effects of PDM on occupational stress, consider a programme for a staff in 25 clinics that operated within the same outpatient hospital (Jackson, 1983). The staff members included nurses, nursing assistants, technicians and clerical workers. The programme simply involved one half of the clinics holding staff meetings at least once per month. Those staff members who had an opportunity to offer input in regular staff meetings had an increased sense of influence and experienced less role stress. In particular, these employees described having less emotional distress and a lower rate of turnover intention (intention to leave the job or profession).

There are several means of ensuring that PDM is successful. First, it is very important that management is committed to the philosophy of PDM. Workers will become discouraged when they offer advice or input and it is ignored by managers. In addition, some supervisors can appear to be interested in PDM but their behaviour is contradictory. For example, consider Eric who is the director of a unit in an organization:

> Having recently attended a workshop on quality, Eric returns to his subordinates and says that all decisions will now be made by teams within the department. The staff in this department might experience disappointment and stress if they spend time in work teams making recommendations and offering input on decisions, only to find that Eric

has maintained an autocratic leadership style and vetoes their suggestions without explanation. Even though he said he was committed to having the staff involved in decision making, he did not behave consistently.

A second note on ensuring that PDM is effective in attempting to alleviate stress involves the kind of decisions that are offered for employee participation. Employees will be most interested in decisions that are important to them (Ivancevich and Matteson, 1980). In other words, managers are encouraged to avoid offering employees a chance to offer input on frivolous matters. In consulting with a variety of work groups, the authors have heard many examples of frivolous decisions (for example, where to put the new drinks machine, what colour waste paper baskets should be purchased, the flavour of ice cream to have at the office holiday party). Employees will feel they have influence only if they are called upon to offer salient input on issues that affect their daily work.

Climate Surveys
A final organizational structure method associated with stress management in workplaces concerns the use of **climate surveys.** Also called attitude surveys, opinion surveys, or employee reaction surveys, these instruments are designed to elicit employee reactions and preferences to assist management in developing action strategies that might improve organizational effectiveness and individual employee satisfaction. The first attempts at this sort of intervention began in the 1950s at Sears, IBM and AT&T. While a more complete discussion of how measurement and evaluation activities might be conducted is presented in Chapter 8, it should be noted that these surveys act as a kind of thermometer with regard to climate in an organization. Thus, a survey can be used 'take the temperature' of the organization and of the employees, and to make comparisons across units, locations, or occupations (Lawler, 1986).

Several specific suggestions have been offered about how to improve a survey effort. For instance, surveys should include well designed questionnaires developed by experienced survey experts. In addition, employees should be allowed to complete the survey anonymously in work time. Also, it is recommended that survey efforts be pursued on a regular basis (for example, annually) so that comparisons can be made and relevant norms developed. After collecting and analysing the data from a survey, it is important to offer feedback on the results to participants. The individuals who represent this feedback should be trained in how to offer feedback effectively. Finally, management must be committed to the entire survey process, including a commitment to follow-up with specific actions based on suggestions offered by employees.

Exhibit 6.1 which follows describes the reaction of a single company to such surveys.

Exhibit 6.1

There's Life Outside Work

Diane Cushman

When plans were being developed in the 1980s to build a $70 million addition to its corporate headquarters complex in downtown Saint Paul, MN, The St. Paul Companies' management asked itself a question: Is this an opportunity to provide additional services or facilities to better serve the needs of our corporate headquarters employees?

The answer was yes, and was confirmed in two employee surveys – if the company would build an on-site child-care centre, many of its 2,500 headquarters employees said they would use it. And, better yet, nationwide statistics showed that such centres produced happier, more productive employees. Even employees who do not have children enrolled in on-site centres tended to feel better about working for employers that support the personal as well as work needs of their employees.

Armed with this information and a desire to be a leading worldwide property and liability insurance company, The St. Paul added to its renovation plans The Children's Center at The St. Paul – a 12,500-square-foot on-site child-care centre licensed for 118 children aged from 6 weeks to 10 years. The centre, which opened in September 1991, has become a cornerstone of the company's family-supportive employee benefits programme.

According to Health and Family Programs Specialist Diane Cushman, 'Employees' lives outside of work can contribute pressures and responsibilities that impact on work productivity. Programmes and services that help employees balance the demands of their personal as well as work lives have a positive impact on employee morale, recruitment and retention. They're not only the right thing to do, they make good business sense.'

The Children's Center is the most visible example of The St. Paul family-supportive benefits, but it plays a comparatively small role among such company benefits as a nationwide child-care resource and referral programme, a broad-brush employee assistance programme, alternative work schedules, an on-site corporate headquarters medical clinic and health and family resource centre, and such options as a vacation purchase plan that enables employees to purchase up to five additional vacation days per year.

The St. Paul is committed to quality in its products, services and systems, and in managing its diverse workforce to achieve the greatest contribution from every employee. 'Family-supportive programs work in concert with these initiatives to achieve excellent service for our customers and the greatest return on our shareholders' investments,' Cushman said.

Headquartered in Saint Paul, MN, The St. Paul Companies is a worldwide insurance organization whose members provide insurance underwriting and insurance brokerage products and services. The St. Paul employs approximately 12,000 people worldwide.

Diane Cushman is associated with The St. Paul Companies, working with Health and Family Programs.

Human Resource Management Systems

There is the potential for employees to experience stress from the time they begin working in a particular setting until the time they leave. Human resource management has been identified as the function within organizations that deals with the many transitions experienced by individuals in organizations. It was suggested in Chapter 4 that the broader focus of human resource management systems beyond career related factors is important in more fully understanding occupational stress. Similarly, the interventions presented in this chapter follow the same pattern; in particular, interventions associated with the following human resource systems are discussed: recruitment and selection, socialization and orientation, goal setting, performance feedback, training, career development and special programmes.

Recruitment and Selection

Recruitment and selection are processes that attract people to an organization and select those people who have the best 'fit' for the job and organizational requirements. In many organizations, recruitment and selection represent a majority of the activities for the human resource management practitioner. Specific stress management strategies have been proposed that focus on recruitment and selection.

In terms of recruitment, one possible strategy is to offer potential employees a **realistic job preview** (RJP). This practice involves exposing perspective employees to the reality of the workplace and the job before they are hired. In this way, RJPs serve as a sort of 'vaccination' that offers the recruit a dose of organizational reality. Having this exposure to the environment before entering acts like a real drug vaccination in which a small amount of the disease is introduced into the individual's body, thus allowing the body to create an immunity. In other words, gaining real experience before beginning a job helps individuals build resistance to unrealistic expectations that might lead to stress after they are hired (Matteson and Ivancevich, 1987).

A number of large American organizations have begun using RJPs, including Texas Instruments, Prudential Life Insurance and the Military Academy (Gibson *et al.*, 1985). RJPs might include both positive and negative information and can be delivered in a variety of formats: booklets, films, videos, oral presentations, job visits and sample work simulations. In addition, some organizations use students on clerkships and cooperative education programmes as a sort of RJP. Little is known about how these various RJP methods help in alleviating stress. What is known is that, in general, RJPs lead to an estimated 30 per cent reduction in turnover. Many managers worry that using RJPs will result in a higher rate of rejection of company offers. Research in this area, however, has indicated that use of RJPs does not lead to a greater rate of rejection of job offers (Wanous, 1980).

One other way in which stress can be reduced for employees involves the selection process. Much has been written in the personnel literature about using selection methods that are reliable and valid. In particular, there is a critical need to match skill and behaviourally based job requirements. If such a match does not occur, it should be obvious that an individual might experience stress. In addition, however, as another means of matching the person and environment, it has been suggested that besides assessing **skills** (as is done in applications and pre-employment interviews), an attempt be made to assess the **needs, values and attitudes** of an applicant. Assessment of these factors would allow for a judgement of whether the person will be a match for a particular position and work environment. Thus, if a person has a low tolerance for ambiguity and he or she is forced to work in a job that called for working alone, the individual might find the job stressful. As a way of making the assessment that is suggested here, many organizations have moved to pre-employment testing. The personality tests used in pre-employment tests offer useful information in deciding whether a person's needs could be met in a particular work environment.

Socialization and Orientation
After entering an organization, an individual is faced with the task of becoming adjusted to the new work environment. This period, often called socialization, has been considered as having great potential for stress. A number of different models describe the process by which an individual enters and becomes adjusted to a work environment. For instance, Matteson and Ivancevich (1987) noted three stages through which individuals must pass as they enter the workplace. The first phase is labelled **getting in**. This phase is said to encompass many of the factors discussed in the preceding section. The second phase involves **breaking in**, and is characterized by the period in which an individual learns about the organization, including co-worker relationships, new job tasks, bureaucratic procedures, role clarification and the evaluation process. Finally, a worker is said to move into the **settling in** phase in which he or she comes to resolve two conflicts: the conflicting demands of work and others in the environment and the conflicting demands of life at work and life outside of work.

Katz (1985) has also attempted to describe the early socialization phase in organizational life. Katz noted that the individual must create a cognitive or mental map of the organizational surroundings and the cast of characters in the work environment. During this period, therefore, the new employee must complete three important tasks: building an organizational role identity, learning about the new boss and other employees, and deciphering the reward system and situational norms.

Considering these two models together, a practitioner can see the components of an intervention that could be used to help an individual deal with stress associated with early socialization. In particular, the practitioner might build programmes and systems that focus on the 'breaking in' phase of the Matteson and Ivancevich model and the three socialization tasks proposed by Katz. These components do comprise many orientation programmes currently in place in organizations. Human resource practitioners should be actively involved in the process of planning and facilitating these programmes aimed at ensuring successful socialization into organizations (Jackson, 1984).

One classic example of a socialization programme is the **anticipatory socialization programme** proposed by Kramer (1974) in the book *Reality Shock*. In this book, Kramer describes a stress management intervention suggested for new employees. This programme is based on the assumption that stress results from the huge gap between the expectation new workers have and the reality of the jobs they encounter. The programme includes four phases. In the first phase, participants are presented with real life incidents that the new worker might encounter on the job. In the book, Kramer describes presenting nurses with a scenario involving a new resident who performs heart massage on an 80 year old patient 'for practice'. As the nurses were presented with this scenario, the instructor attempted to provide counter arguments to their reactions (for example, if the resident does not practice, how will she learn the procedure?). In the second phase of the programme, the participants are asked what they could do to offer alternative solutions given that impossible conditions exist. In addition, phase two includes participants interviewing veterans in the field to see how they might respond to the scenarios. The third phase of the programme allows the participants to gain a 'realistic baseline' of expectations by exposing them to panels of co-workers whom they would encounter in the field. In the case of nurses, the panel included medical doctors and nursing supervisors. Finally in the fourth phase of the programme, the participants are taught theories and techniques of conflict resolution and negotiation.

Goal Setting

Throughout the previous chapters, we have emphasized the importance of role ambiguity and role confusion as components of occupational stress. One intervention technique that is helpful in dealing with these problems is goal setting. Stated simply, goal setting involves determining specific standards of performance that will be sought. The goal setting process assists in the reduction of stress in four ways (Locke and Latham, 1984): first, the employee receives a sense of satisfaction when a goal is achieved; secondly, the process of being involved in individual action can be reassuring; thirdly, the goal setting process gives the employee a sense of continually moving towards a defined target; and fourthly, goal setting is said to reduce the feelings of uncertainty that an employee might experience with regard to performance evaluation. Much has been written about what makes the goal setting process successful. To summarize, the goal setting process is most likely to be successful if a goal is challenging but not too difficult. In addition, it is important that a goal be written and that the goal setting process include agreement between the employee and supervisor about how performance will be measured and when performance will be reviewed.

A well known system of goal setting is **management by objectives** (MBO) which was developed by Drucker. MBO is a philosophy and system in which the actions to be achieved and the process of monitoring progress are clearly defined before performance begins. MBO starts with a mission statement that defines the group's purpose. From this mission statement, workers identify a series of goals that will be attempted to achieve the mission. Finally for each goal, a series of action steps or objectives are planned. While MBO is very popular in organizational use, the system is not without problems (Ivancevich and Matteson, 1980). In particular, the very system that has been designed to alleviate stress by reducing ambiguity and uncertainty often causes stress by pushing workers to complete large amounts of paper work and to have additional meetings with supervisors.

Performance Feedback
Receiving feedback on performance has long been understood to affect motivation and satisfaction, and this premise is especially true in work. We have already outlined the ways in which faulty performance feedback systems, especially performance appraisal forms and evaluation forms, can lead to stress. Not only are these systems linked to stress, but they are closely associated with burnout (Jackson, 1984). Despite the fact that most people in management understand the importance of doing performance evaluation and appraisal, it is not usually listed either as a top priority or a favoured activity for most management staff. Some experts have suggested that this reluctance to offer performance feedback to employees is linked to several different factors. This reluctance could be due to the fact that the task of judging others is unfamiliar and uncomfortable for many people. In addition, some managers and supervisors may avoid the task of conducting performance reviews because they have had a bad experience with the process or they have not been trained in how to conduct such reviews properly. Finally, many managers comment that perform-ance review is not a primary task of their job. One supervisor noted that he did not get a pay rise for the number of job reviews that he finished but he did get paid when output on the assembly line increased.

Several intervention strategies have been offered for dealing with these difficulties. One suggestion involves providing training to supervisors focused on understanding how performance evaluation systems operate in general and within the human resource management systems of an organization in particular. In addition, this training would teach managers to communicate with employees about performance in behaviourally specific terms.

Another possibility is to consider obtaining rating information from a variety of sources. In the preceding section, it was suggested that verifiable goals be set before performance evaluation begins. Given such goals are measurable, they could be used as one source of information that would not involve subjective judgement on the part of the supervisor (for example, the sales representative increased sales calls by 20 per cent, the counsellor decreased the average number of sessions for therapy clients by 1.5 sessions). Other sources of information besides the supervisor might include co-workers or customers. Several organizations have begun asking for customer/client satisfaction information as a way of evaluating an individual's or a work group's performance. Similarly there have been groups (especially those utilizing principles of TQM) who have moved to systems that include peer feedback. One group, for instance, has a set time twice per year where the staff takes a half day away from work to conduct performance evaluation. During this half day session, each member of the team takes a turn being in the 'hot seat' and having all other members of the staff offer feedback. This method has met with initially positive results. As a side note, however, anecdotal accounts of the process of setting up this system indicate that many employees were very fearful of the process and offered a great deal of resistance as the programme was initiated.

As a final suggestion with regard to performance feedback interventions to deal with stress, one might consider the focus of the evaluation. Ivancevich and Matteson (1980) described the focus of feedback sessions as being either judgemental or developmental. They argue that traditional evaluation systems have been judgemental in that they focus on judging the past behaviour of an individual. Developmental evaluation, on the other hand, is focused on an employee's development in the future, not the past. Several organizations have begun to move from using judgemental evaluation systems to developmental ones. For instance, one corporation has instituted an employee development programme that includes requiring each supervisor to have a discussion with all of his or her employees regarding their direction and development on an annual basis. Interestingly, these meetings must follow the employees' performance reviews. Similarly, this organization has created a new category of evaluation for managers: the category labelled 'employee development' involves a rating by the manager's supervisor on how well the manager provides performance feedback.

Training

Training has been identified as an important component of interventions to deal with occupational stress (Sauter *et al.*, 1990). Several areas of training should be pursued with regard to stress management: helping individuals cope, teaching managers about the importance of job design, and informing workers about the incidence of psychological disorders and the job factors that increase the risk of psychological disorders. One criticism noted in the introduction to this chapter is that many organizations attempt to rely solely on stress management training as a way to intervene. It is important to remember that stress management training alone does not sufficiently deal with the problem. Instead, such training should be part of a larger intervention strategy.

For instance, Murphy and Hurrell (1987) described an intervention in which a stress management programme was built into a larger organizational system. A department was presented that had employees who were extremely dissatisfied, with low morale, and who were experiencing high levels of stress. In this intervention, the practitioners began with a workshop on stress management. The leaders of the workshop then provided information to department management regarding the kind of stress factors reported by employees. The data from these reports were used to develop a stressor evaluation survey administered to the entire organization. A committee of representatives from the psychology department and management reviewed the data from this survey and made recommendations about how the organization might respond with specific actions. This approach is unique in that it did not legitimize the existence of stress in the organization. Rather, the entire process fostered awareness about the nature and scope of the stress in the organization. Finally, the process was a useful intervention because the participants in the stress management workshop were able to learn valuable coping skills.

Career Development

The organizational career development model presented in Chapter 4 outlined the responsibilities of both the individual and the organization with regard to career development. In particular, it was noted that the organization is responsible for certain activities including recruitment, selection, placement, development, succession planning and promotions. These organizational responsibilities do not operate in a vacuum, however. In fact, there are a number of factors in our society that make the entire process of career management much more complex than in years past. Career management for organizations was at one time characterized by traditional career ladders defined by tenure and performance. Today, however, a more advanced conceptualization of career development is needed because of a variety of factors: structural changes within organizations (for example, elimination of middle management in many organizations), demographic changes in the workforce (for example, more working parents and dual career families), and changes in the nature of work (for example, rapidly advancing technology that leads to skill obsolescence and plateauing).

These factors have implications for the way organizations respond to career development stress experienced by workers. For instance, workers are becoming aware of the need to take responsibility for their own careers. They realize that people can no longer simply wait for the 'organization' to surprise them with a promotion. Instead, workers in the next several decades will need to monitor opportunities for job changes inside and outside of their organizations along with developing skills that will leave them ready for career transitions. Similarly, organizations can no longer assume that every worker aspires to be a president of the company by making all of the appropriate stops at key positions on the rise to the top. Instead factors outside of work (for example, family, dual careers, interest in balance between work and non-work life) will lead workers to look for opportunities to create new job situations and pursue non-traditional career paths.

All of these factors taken together should lead to the conclusion that new and creative intervention strategies will be important in helping workers deal with career development stress. This task can seem very difficult for practitioners charged with creating these programmes. However, Kaye (1982) suggests several advantages for an organization as career development intervention strategies are undertaken: increased employee skill building, improved talent matching, individual revitalization, problem identification and increased goal commitment. Several organizations have attempted to create career programmes that begin to address some of these needs. For instance, Polaroid Corporation has a programme that includes the integration of organizational needs into the career planning system. In particular, the system involves a training programme that helps employees understand the value of lateral moves, identify skills that transfer between job families, take initiative in making career contacts, and use the company job posting system.

Another organization (Lawrence Livermore National Laboratories) has designed a career programme that does not include traditional workshop training. Instead, the company maintains a career resource centre with over 3,000 resources focused on a wide variety of topics such as educational opportunities, career planning, the world of work and management. The resource centre also includes a computerized information bank on career planning and the developmental stages of careers. Finally, the materials include a series of self-study instruments and resources that give information about off-site training opportunities (Ferrini and Parker, 1978).

As a final example of a career planning system to aid workers in coping with stress, one of the authors has been involved in the development of a career programme in the Michigan Division of the Dow Chemical Company. This programme includes a combination of the features described in the two programmes above. Participants begin the process by completing a series of vocational interest, ability and personality tests. They then participate in a workshop that involves interpretation of their tests along with an introduction to several models of career and life planning and to the resources that are available to them as employees. These resources include a resource library, a computerized career planning programme (which includes information about how skills, interests and values match with specific jobs in the company) and ongoing training and continuing education. Finally, each participant meets individually with a psychologist to discuss the results of the assessment and develop an action approach for career and life planning. This programme is beginning to become part of the other human resource management systems in that it is introduced as a part of orientation and serves as the foundation for the employee development programme that includes meetings between each employee and their supervisors to discuss ongoing development.

Special Programmes

In addition to the programmes mentioned above, several other specialized programmes have been developed for dealing with stress in the workplace. These programmes are labelled differently across organizations, but in general they are referred to as employee assistance programmes (EAP) and health awareness programmes. The development of such programmes is traced to 1919 when Marian Brockway (a well known New York City nurse) was hired by Metropolitan Insurance Company to counsel female employees who were experiencing stress managing the responsibilities and demands of families and jobs (McLeod, 1985). Since that time, the number of programmes of this sort has grown exponentially. For instance, in 1945 there were six EAPs in the United States. By 1973, this number had grown to 500, and in 1980 there were a reported 4,400 programmes (Preston and Bierman, 1985).

The primary aim of an EAP is to decrease the effect that personal problems might have on productivity (Sauter *et al.*, 1990). Initially, these programmes focused on alcohol and other chemical dependency issues, especially among blue collar workers. More recently EAPs have come to be inclusive in the focus of issues and in the employee groups who are served (Nahrwold, 1987). The actual source of sponsorship of EAPs varies greatly across organizations to include unions, medical centres, human resource management departments, employee relations, and training and development. The services that are offered across EAPs involve telephone hotlines, short-term counselling, referral and follow-ups (Walsh, 1982).

Health awareness programmes have been developed as an extension of EAPS aimed at the prevention of illness through education and the advocacy of good health. The services offered in health awareness programmes include nutrition, fitness and exercise, smoking cessation, and health risk appraisals. Such programmes are not limited to huge corporations; smaller organizations also offer programmes often by contracting with local community agencies to provide services that promote health (for example, hospitals, churches, gyms, local YM/WCAs).

While programmes of this type have continued to grow in popularity, very little systematic evaluation has been conducted (Murphy and Hurrell, 1987). One trend is a consistent pattern for both EAPs and health programmes to move towards prevention. Several authors have offered other suggestions for the future direction of this field. For instance, they note that future directions of the programmes are to focus on prevention, to continue to help individuals in learning coping skills, to increase the method of evaluation, and to professionalize the administration of such programmes (Walsh, 1982).

Physical Qualities

As a final category of stress intervention strategies, consider the physical environmental stressors described in Chapter 4. It is usually beyond the skill and job responsibility of human resource management practitioners to deal with the technical difficulties encountered in the workplace. These interventions might be better left to engineering experts. There are, however, two general principles regarding stress management in relation to physical aspects of work that the human resource practitioner should consider. The first is that there are multiple ways to deal with the physical environment stressors encountered. For example, a practitioner might alter the environment to deal with the stressor (for example, decrease the noise level, cut the light glare). Other strategies involve protecting people from the stressor (for example, use tinted glass or earplugs) or changing procedures of operation (for example, shorter and more frequent breaks, waiving customary dress requirements, providing a place to escape).

As a second principle, it should be noted that the consultant does not need to be the expert in solving the physical stress factor problems. Instead, it has been recommended that practitioners consider the person in the job itself as the best source of information about how to alleviate the conditions that are causing the stress. Thus, a strategy would be to use the expertise of the persons in the job to generate ideas and solutions about how to improve the working conditions that are causing stress. As a means of implementing this principle, the practitioner might consider conducting focus groups in which workers are offered an opportunity to discuss those aspects of the work environment they experience as stressful and to brainstorm suggestions about how these physical stressors could be handled.

A Final Note on Intervention

In reviewing the intervention strategies presented here, it is admittedly overwhelming to consider how one might plan an intervention effort to help workers deal with stress. In conceptualizing the most effective plan of attack, it might be useful to consider three components of intervention.

The first component is labelled **process areas of expertise**, that is, the process or skills the practitioner can use in making an intervention. Examples of process areas of expertise for a human resource management or counselling practitioner are given in Table 6.3. A second component to consider is the **content areas of expertise** that might be used in intervention. Content areas refer to the topics or subjects about which a practitioner is qualified or willing to consult. Examples of content areas of expertise are given in Table 6.4. Having identified the first two areas of expertise, the practitioner can then identify the third area: **supplementary areas of expertise**. This component refers to resources that are available in an organization or in the community that might serve to supplement the resources the practitioner has available. Examples of supplementary resources might include contracting with a local

Table 6.3   *Skills areas for practitioners (process areas of expertise)*

Skills areas	Examples
Training for managers and employees Developing and facilitating workshops and seminars to improve work-related skills.	• Creating a workshop for managers on identifying substance abuse among employees. • Presenting a programme on preparing for retirement.
Consultation with managers Offering expertise and advice to managers as they deal with individual employees or organization-wide policies and procedures.	• Meeting with management as they attempt to assess why 90 per cent of women sales representatives leave the company. • Talk with a supervisor about how to deal with a problem performer.
Development of wellness promotion programmes Establishing health and wellness workshops, materials and activities.	• Contracting with the local hospital to conduct smoking cessation workshops for employees. • Developing a brochure on healthy eating tips for employees who travel for the company.
Individual counselling and coaching Working with individuals to help them develop coping skills to deal with performance and other work-related problems.	• Assisting a secretary in developing assertiveness skills in dealing with clients. • Talking with a supervisor about running more productive meetings.
Specialized counselling Offering individual assistance in dealing with interpersonal problems, personal issues, or situational difficulties that may lead to problems in work.	• Offering job search counselling to outplaced employees. • Talking with a family that is being relocated to another country.
Group facilitation Serving as a leader or facilitator of some group activity or ongoing counselling group.	• Leading a team building retreat for a work group. • Facilitating a focus group on minority employee concerns.
Referral Providing information to an individual or group about resources inside or outside of the organization.	• Assisting an employee in understanding insurance benefits. • Offering information about chemical dependency treatment programmes in the community.

Table 6.3   *cont.*

Skills areas	Examples
Research Conducting surveys or related research activities for use in organizational decision making.	• Tracking employee use of organization medical and EAP services. • Analysing results of a survey about management practices in different departments.
Production of educational materials Preparing written materials or audiovisual programmes that focus on issues of concern to employees.	• Writing an article on balancing work/family life for the company newsletter. • Appearing as a 'guest' on an organizational television programme on employee stress.
Advocacy Serving as an advocate for an individual/group who is/are having conflict with the organization.	• Meeting individually with an employee who is filing sexual harassment charges. • Suggesting to management that the parental leave policy be expanded to include fathers.
Testing and assessment Administering and interpreting psychological tests or related instruments that aid an individual or the organization.	• Providing career interest and value testing for employees as they plan their careers. • Interpreting personality test results for members of a work group as they attempt to improve group cohesion.

hospital to conduct wellness seminars for employees or working with an organization's communications department to develop a brochure on effective performance reviews.

Identifying these three areas of expertise will allow the practitioner to see many options that are available in designing an intervention strategy. As an example, imagine that a practitioner encounters the following situation. As part of a major reorganization, a company was forced to lay off about 20 per cent of its workforce. A number of stress-related factors were observed. Many employees had spouses or family members who were laid-off in the reorganization. In addition, stress was reported by employees who remained in the workplace because of fear that more jobs could be eliminated at any minute and because of the increased workload for employees who remained.

Table 6.4   *Examples of content areas of expertise*

Content areas of expertise	Examples
People skills	Communication; motivation; active listening; selling; negotiating; assertiveness.
Group dynamics	Group cohesion; social support; managing conflict; dealing with diversity; special population concerns; leadership.
Performance issues	Job redesign; job enrichment; job rotation; performance appraisal; performance feedback; employee evaluation.
Wellness	Exercise/fitness; smoking cessation; chemical use/abuse; weight control; biofeedback/relaxation; safety concerns.
Extraorganizational factors	Dual careers; marriage and family; relocation; retirement; elder/child care; life values.
Career development	Career stages; job search skills; outplacement; plateauing; mentoring; socialization.
Assessment	Selection/placement; vocational testing; health/life style; survey design/administration; data analysis; personality testing.
Testing and development	Designing training; facilitating groups; evaluating effectiveness; employee development; continuing education; orientation.
Organizational dynamics	Organizational structure; organizational climate; managing change; mergers; acquisitions; lay-offs and downsizing.

Using the areas of expertise distinction outlined above, the practitioner in this situation might design the following intervention:

- Content areas of expertise:
  - Assertiveness
  - Job redesign
  - Wellness
  - Job outplacement
- Process areas of expertise:
  - Training
  - Individual counselling
  - Research
  - Production of educational materials
- Supplementary areas of expertise
  - Community mental health clinic
  - Local displaced worker programme
  - Company's communication department

Examining these possible resources, the practitioner might combine them as the following interventions:

1 Develop training programmes for managers on how to help work groups reorganize and redesign work given the reduced staff.
2 Work with the communication department to publish tips on coping with stress and wellness in the company's newsletter.
3 Meet with the individual employees who have been outplaced to identify outplacement resources in the community they can use in their job searches.
4 Hire staff from the community mental health centre to lead support groups at lunch hours for employees who have spouses who have been laid-off.
5 Aid the organization's management in designing an employee attitude survey to assess areas of greatest stress for employees; analysing and interpreting the results as management does strategic planning.

In this way, the practitioner could have designed a multi-dimensional approach to intervene in helping these employees deal with stress. Practitioners are cautioned to avoid feeling over-whelmed by how to respond to stress problems in the work environment. By reviewing the areas of expertise outlined in this section, the practitioner might be surprised by how many possible intervention resources are available.

7
Designing Effective Evaluations

Practitioners developing interventions for occupational stress need to understand the critical role that evaluation plays in designing and evaluating the intervention. As has been noted in previous chapters, interventions often are developed based on data from employees or an employer regarding occupational stress among workers. In addition, a key question for any organization is whether there is an adequate 'return' on the investment made in interventions for occupational stress. Both of these questions can be answered effectively with carefully designed evaluations. This chapter will briefly discuss issues around the use of evaluations and will describe measures that assess both individuals and workplaces. We should note at the outset that a single chapter cannot do justice to the many issues involved in designing effective evaluations; the interested reader is encouraged to consult texts on evaluation research and programme evaluation for more information (Kosecoff and Fink, 1982: Stufflebeam and Shinkfield, 1985; Worthen and Sanders, 1987; Patton, 1990; Shadish et al., 1991).

Issues in Evaluations

There are several key issues to be considered in designing evaluations. The first is the **purpose** of the evaluation. While determining the effectiveness of a particular intervention is a fairly clear purpose, surveying workers within an organization regarding their experience of stress is not as clear. The latter could lead to asking questions regarding work climate, the work environment, supervisor–employee relationships, or many other aspects of occupational stress. Thus, a practitioner must have a clear statement of the purposes of evaluation prior to designing and conducting it. An example of this clear purpose might be, 'What is the effect on retention of offering in-house career counselling for middle-level managers?'

Equally important as the purpose of a study is its intended **audience**. The design of an evaluation will be dictated in part by its purpose, but it will also be influenced by its audience. For example, if an evaluation of a particular workplace intervention is being conducted, there are several types of measures that could be included. Data which speak to the needs and concerns of the intended audience will be more persuasive than data which do not. So, for example, top level management may be more persuaded by outcome data which reveal lower inpatient health care costs for employees who received a smoking cessation intervention than by data from the same programme which suggest that employees also experienced improved self-esteem when they stopped smoking. Returning to our previous question – whether a career counselling programme can be shown to retain middle level managers who might formerly have moved elsewhere – then the company will have saved the costs of replacing these workers.

A third critical question concerns the **resources** that can be placed into the evaluation study. Such studies can range from very costly, as might occur if interviewers were hired to interview individually employees in their homes, to cost effective, as might be the case with pencil and paper measures developed by the company for its own purposes. The resources available must be clarified ahead of time.

In the special case of an evaluation conducted to evaluate the effectiveness of an intervention, the practitioner must be careful to define the criteria for success since there is a wide range of criteria that could indicate the 'success' of a particular intervention. Criteria could be primarily 'institutional' in nature, such as measures of absenteeism or turnover. Criteria can also be primarily 'individual' in nature, such as measures of mental health or job satisfaction. There are criteria that reflect a utilitarian return on the company's investment, such as cost–benefit analyses. There are also criteria that are more humanitarian in nature, such as occupational stress measures.

It should also be noted that occupational stress interventions have several 'constituencies'. Thus, practitioners may work within the organization or outside the organization, and evaluations may be designed from either of these two vantage points. If practitioners are internal to the organization, then the degree to which they can advocate for interventions is somewhat limited since resources are controlled by the organization and the practitioners' own power to 'make things happen' within the organization may be limited by their role. Practitioners outside an organization, hired for a particular function, may have more freedom and may be in a position that is more persuasive with regard to resources. However, some principles apply regardless of the position of the practitioners: be clear about the risks of the intervention as well as its potential contributions, define objectives and expectations of success, and clarify roles in recommending changes based on the intervention.

Having all of this material as a background, let us turn to a discussion of methods by which practitioners can assess both individuals and organizations.

Individual Assessment

Many times, a practitioner wishes to understand the unique experience of certain individuals within the organization. This assessment might target overall experience of occupational stress or burnout, or might consider concomitants of stress such as depression, physical health symptoms, or coping. In considering the effects of a stress management intervention, the practitioner is most likely to want to obtain an assessment of the individual's experience after the intervention in order to determine the positive (or negative) effects of the intervention. Thus, individual assessment serves as a critical component in establishing the effectiveness of any stress management intervention.

Physical Health

There are many measures of overall health and functions which can provide a baseline of employee 'health'. One such measure is the Duke Health Profile (Parkerson *et al.*, 1990). This measure contains 17 items used to calculate six health measures (physical health, mental health, social health, general health, perceived health and self-esteem) as well as four functional measures (anxiety, depression, pain and disability). Thus, for a small investment of time, the practitioner can obtain a range of information about the employee.

The Duke Health Profile possesses adequate reliability and validity, and can serve as a general measure of 'health' for considering outcomes of interventions as well as a baseline measure. An example of its use would be to measure the overall effects of an intervention reducing occupational stress on employee health. While such an intervention might have many types of effects, its impact on employee health might be of particular interest in a cost–benefit analysis. The Duke Health Profile can serve as such an overall measure of health effects.

Measuring Stress

It is likely that a practitioner will wish to have an assessment of the levels of occupational stress among employees. Such an assessment targets the occupational stress experienced by workers within an organization and may provide the most direct test of the effectiveness of an intervention designed to reduce occupational stress. Although several such measures are available, we will describe the Occupational Stress Inventory (OSI) as an example of an especially useful measure.

The **Occupational Stress Inventory** (Osipow and Spokane, 1987) was developed to provide measures of occupational stress applicable across a variety of job settings. The measure considers three domains of occupational stress; occupational roles, personal strains and coping responses. We will discuss each of these domains individually to illustrate them as aspects of occupational stress that a practitioner will want to target in assessment.

Occupational roles that are assessed by the OSI include role overload, role insufficiency, role ambiguity, role boundary, responsibility and physical environment. The reader will recall that in Chapter 4 these aspects of the work environment contribute to occupational stress. The term 'role boundary', for example, refers to the degree to which the individual experiences conflicting role demands in a work setting. Thus, the occupational roles that are assessed by the OSI are those associated with occupational stress in a variety of jobs.

The second domain is **personal strains**: vocational strain, psychological strain, interpersonal strain and physical strain. All of these scale titles are self-descriptive except for vocational strain: this scale measures the degree to which a worker is having difficulty with work quality or productivity, including negative attitudes toward his and her job. All of these areas of occupational stress have also be considered previously in this book as both symptoms and 'causes' of occupational stress.

The third domain is a set of four scales measuring **coping resources**: recreation, self-care, social support and rational/cognitive coping. These scales consider the means by which a person copes with life stressors. The items are worded generally; that is, they do not pertain only to work stressors, but rather assess how frequently a person is able to access coping resources. For example, one item is 'I spend enough time in recreational activities to satisfy my needs.'

The OSI was based on theoretical models of occupational stress and is exemplary in the way in which it considers both role strains and psychological strains as well as coping resources. Because these three domains are sampled, it is possible for the practitioner to consider both stress and coping within one profile. As mentioned earlier in this book, the presence of coping resources serves to 'buffer' against the negative effects of high levels of stress (see Osipow and Davis, 1988). Thus, having information on stress and coping will enable the practitioner to obtain the most accurate picture of occupational stress.

Chapter 8 presents several additional examples of handouts that can give a measure of occupational stress. For example, handout 2 allows measurement of stressful life events and handout 7 considers the overall level of occupational stress.

Coping Responses

Although coping resources are included in the OSI, and in other stress measures as well, it may be important for a practitioner to measure directly a person's coping responses. Theoretically, a stress management intervention might work by increasing a worker's confidence that coping would be effective, and thus increase his or her coping responses although not increasing coping resources per se.

Carver *et al.* (1989) have developed a measure of coping styles that assesses a person's use of ten types or categories of coping, six of which are 'adaptive' in that the person is actively working at coping with the stressor and four of which are 'non-adaptive' in that the person is withdrawing from the stressor. This categorization may be helpful in and of itself. The ten types and their definitions are contained in Table 7.1.

Research conducted by Carver *et al.* on their scale revealed that persons in stressful situations in which control was not possible used more denial, more focus on emotion, more disengagement (both behavioural and emotional) and less active coping. Interestingly, persons who scored high on a measure of optimism (similar in definition to the sense of coherence) were more likely to cope actively, and were more likely to use acceptance and positive reinterpretation. A practitioner might find such a measure of coping helpful for determining pre- to post-intervention changes or for better understanding a particular person's responses to a stressful work situation.

Self-monitoring

In previous chapters, we presented use of diary methods to uncover stressful situations. Any means by which a worker monitors or measures a particular behaviour or situation for himself or herself would be categorized as self-monitoring. Observing and recording can be undertaken to keep a record of thoughts and feelings, the frequency of particular behaviours, or rating scales for the intensity of an event. A diary of thoughts and

Table 7.1 *Coping categories and sample items*

Coping categories	Sample items
Active coping: Making a plan of action and following it.	'I concentrate my efforts on doing something about the problem.'
Suppression of competing activities: Not being distracted by other thoughts or activities.	'I focus on dealing with this problem, and if necessary let other things slide a little.'
Positive reinterpretation: Try to grow as a person as a result of this experience.	'I try to see it in a different light, to make it seem more positive.'
Acceptance: Get used to the idea that it happened.	'I accept that this has happened and that it can't be changed.'
Seeking emotional social support: Discuss feelings with someone.	'I try to get emotional support from friends or relatives.'
Seeking instrumental social support: Get advice from someone.	'I talk to someone to find out more about the situation.'
Denial: Telling yourself 'this isn't real.'	'I refuse to believe that it has happened.'
Focus on emotions: Think about how awful you feel.	'I get upset, and am really aware of it.'
Behavioural disengagement: Give up trying to reach your goal.	'I give up the attempt to get what I want.'
Mental disengagement: Daydream about things other than this.	'I sleep more than usual.'

feelings might be useful when the employee is interested in discovering the antecedents and/or consequences of an event. These are the behaviours and feelings that come before and/or after an event, that is, the context of the event. For example, an employee might report periodic episodes of tension headaches at work, but have no association between these headaches and particular events. A diary such as is illustrated in Table 7.2 might suggest to the employee that her interactions with her supervisor serve as a trigger for the stress headache.

Another way to use a diary is to record the frequency of certain events. An employee who is using a diary might keep track of the number of times a behaviour occurs, such as complaining about a supervisor to her friends. Alternatively, the duration of an event can be recorded, as time in minutes spent on the telephone or answering letters.

The last method is to use some type of rating scale to record the intensity of an event or situation. An employee might wish to use a simple 7-point scale, where 1 = 'Not at all stressed' and 7 = 'Extremely stressed', to evaluate how stressed he or she is during a typical week at work. This type of chart might reveal that particular days or times of day are most stressful, and the

Table 7.2   *Examples of monitoring – structured diary*

Antecedents	Behaviours	Consequences
Monday morning: my supervisor ignored me in the lift.	I got angry with her and complained to my friends.	Anger, stress, headache.
Wednesday afternoon: I made a comment in our weekly meeting that I thought was good, but my supervisor disagreed with what I said.	I said some stupid things in the meeting, and complained about her to my friends later that afternoon.	I felt bad, and I got a headache.
Friday morning: I scheduled a meeting with my supervisor to have a performance assessment.	I worried all day about what she would say.	I was upset and got a headache.

Table 7.3   *Rating scale use Average Day*

Day:	Time: 8.00	9.00	10.00	11.00	12.00	1.00	2.00	3.00	4.00	5.00
Monday	1	2	3	3	2	5	5	4	4	3
Tuesday	3	3	2	6	5	4	4	3	4	3
Wednesday	4	4	3	5	3	4	6	4	3	2
Thursday	4	5	6	7	7	6	5	6	7	3
Friday	5	6	5	4	6	7	7	6	5	4

1 = Not at all stressed; 7 = Extremely stressed

employee can then consider what the events are of that time which are causing this degree of stress. Table 7.3 provides an example of the use of this scale for an employee. First, he begins each day less stressed than he ends it. Secondly, his stress level builds through the week. Thirdly, he seems to experience most stress during the middle of his days. It would take an event diary to determine if there are certain events correlated with these patterns or if these patterns represent an overall stress response.

Although the purposes of self-monitoring and the target behaviours or feelings would vary, there are several principles that apply to this assessment method. The most obvious is that the method must be easy to use and convenient to carry around, since it is essential that recording be made at the time of the event. It is not possible to remember accurately how stressed one was during the day at the end of the day nor what events led to what consequences. A second principle is to be clear about the target of monitoring. The behaviour being counted or the emotion being rated for intensity must be clearly defined so that an accurate record can be kept. A third principle is that the record must be interpreted accurately. It is best to look for patterns in the record across a series of days or even weeks, since when one begins monitoring behaviour there is a tendency to have a behaviour change when it is being observed.

Organization Assessment

Organization assessment considers the experience of an organization more generally. Such measures often are more 'molar'; that is, they reflect the combined experience of many persons and thus serve only as a rough indicator of the experience of the individual people within an organization. However, they do reflect an organization or system as a whole, and thus should be considered in evaluating the problems of occupational stress within an organization or the effectiveness of any intervention designed to prevent or reduce such stress.

Absenteeism and Turnover

Throughout this book, we have noted that absenteeism and turnover are often associated with occupational stress and, especially, burnout. In some cases, these behaviours were identified as symptoms of stress. In addition, absenteeism and turnover were presented as 'costs' of occupational stress in the workplace. Finally, we noted that absenteeism and turnover can represent attempts to cope with occupational stress, since both behaviours allow an individual to 'withdraw' from stressful situations.

In this chapter, we wish to emphasize that absenteeism and turnover are two measures that can monitor the effectiveness of stress management interventions. These measures seem especially important because of the 'bottom line' cost savings that can be obtained for interventions which reduce either absenteeism or turnover.

In considering **turnover** as a measure, it is important to be aware of the real costs associated with any employee leaving a job (see Muchinsky and Tuttle, 1979; Mobley, 1982). These costs include the money it will take to recruit, select and train a new employee. Additional costs are seen in the decrease of productivity as the new employee replaces an experienced employee and in the increased amount of time it takes to supervise a new employee. Despite the literature on turnover, however, we have little empirical data to support assertions that stress management programmes reduce job turnover (Murphy, 1985). One of the few examples of these studies (Gray-Toft, 1980) reported that lower turnover was seen for workers on a hospice unit who had participated in a stress counselling programme compared with other health care workers in the same hospital.

In measuring **absenteeism**, the rate is usually based on the number of days an employee is away or absent from the job. However, Matteson and Ivancevich (1987) noted that absenteeism can be a legitimate reality when people are ill and not able to work. However, the other type of absenteeism that occurs when workers are not ill or take unnecessary time after an illness has ended is problematic. Not only does absenteeism affect productivity, it can also serve to reduce an employee's level of motivation and thus exacerbate already existing problems.

Similar to turnover, while there are a number of studies that have focused on absenteeism, few research reports have examined the effects of stress management programmes on reducing absenteeism. In fact, Murphy (1985) reported in his literature review that no studies had linked stress management with absenteeism reduction, although secondary accounts of such research were available.

Turnover and absenteeism are not independent criteria: many people show higher absence rates before they actually leave. Turnover may be a gradual process (people begin to think about leaving and to evaluate options before they quit). Turnover might also be determined by employees' assessment of their ability to find other employment. Given these observations, measurement of turnover might best focus on intent to leave and not actual leaving. Attempting to reduce turnover might also backfire when short-term reduction in turnover does not fit with long-term organizational objectives. For example, consider the situation that occurs when an organization might like to see poor-performing employees leave. In this situation, turnover could be functional for the organization. Hence, a better focus of intervention might be on the intention of good, competent employees to leave.

Job Satisfaction

Research that has considered the effects of stress on job-related variables has yielded inconclusive results. Some studies have found that certain stressors in certain situations improve job performance and job satisfaction and work stress while other research has indicated that stress can lead to decreases in job performance and job satisfaction (McGrath, 1976; Beehr and Newman, 1978). The relationship between job satisfaction is further complicated when individual differences are considered. As an example, Walshok (1981) conducted an extensive study examining the impact of stress on men and women in the same blue collar jobs. The results indicated that women and men showed very different levels of job satisfaction for the same jobs.

Throughout the previous chapters, low job satisfaction has been identified as a symptom of occupational stress. In terms of evaluating the effectiveness of stress management interventions, job satisfaction might also be useful as an outcome measure. However, it is difficult to determine the best way of measuring the construct. In some cases, direct behavioural assessments are used to determine job satisfaction. Examples of such behavioural measures might include determining frequency of absences, number of employees who leave (turnover), or the number of grievances reported. The rationale for using these measures is that by assessing these variables, one can make inferences about an individual's level of satisfaction with work.

The alternative method for assessing job satisfaction is to use self-report instruments. Several different self-report measures are available (for example, Job Description Inventory [JDI]; Faces Scale, Minnesota Satisfaction Questionnaire [MSQ]). As an example, the MSQ consists of 100 items that assess workers' satisfaction with 20 different aspects of the work environment. Each of the 20 reinforcing aspects of work is associated with a psychological need: ability utilization, achievement, activity, advancement, authority, company policies and practices, compensation, co-workers, creativity, independence, moral values, recognition, responsibility, security, social service, social status, supervision-human relations, supervision-technical variety and working conditions. Employees rate each item on a scale ranging from 'Not Satisfied' to 'Extremely Satisfied'. Individuals' scores can be computed to yield an index of the level of job satisfaction. In addition, aggregate scores can be computed to yield group scores. These group scores can be used to compare job satisfaction before and after an intervention or to make comparisons among work groups within an organization.

Work Climate
In Chapter 4, we discussed the impact that organizational variables can have on an employee's perception of occupational stress. In particular, we said that an organization's structure, territory, and climate can be related to occupational stress and burnout. However, the difficulty with using work climate as an outcome

measure in evaluating stress management effectiveness stems from the lack of clarity with which climate is defined. You might recall from Chapter 4 that climate might be described as the 'feel' that characterizes certain organizations. Attempts to operationalize this concept have focused on many different factors, including physical environment, attitudes, behaviours, interaction of people, policies and goals. As might be expected, there has been great criticism of the usefulness of the work climate construct. Much of the criticism has been aimed at the methods by which reliable and valid measurement of climate can be completed (Gibson *et al.*, 1979). These measurement difficulties have led to a lack of consistency in research conducted on work climate.

Despite these problems, work climate has been used to measure stress management effectiveness. For instance, in one study (Ivancevich and Lyon, 1972), hospital personnel were asked to make ratings on climate (for example, intimacy, product orientation, esprit, aloofness) in terms of how their needs were satisfied for each aspect. Results indicated that different aspects of the work climate were more important for specific subgroups of employees. For instance, nurses associated need satisfaction with a climate high in 'esprit' while administrators associated need satisfaction with a climate high in 'consideration'. A practitioner could determine the areas that are most important to different groups of employees with regard to stress management.

Several other standardized measures of work climate are also available. The **Work Inventory Scale** (Moos *et al.*, 1974) measures dimensions of the social structure of a workplace. These dimensions are believed to be predictive of the climate of the workplace and, in turn, worker satisfaction or adjustment. Another example of a work climate measure is the **Stress Diagnostic Survey** (Ivancevich and Matteson, 1980). This instrument includes 25 items that describe different aspects of the work environment. Using a 7-point scale, the respondents are asked to make a rating that ranges from 'never a stressor in my job' to 'always a stressor in my job'. Scores are computed for 7 subscales: organizational climate, organizational structure, organizational territory, technology, leader influence, lack of cohesion and group support. A final example of a measure of climate is the **Osipow Stress Inventory** (OSI) (Osipow and Spokane, 1987). As we described earlier in this chapter, this instrument includes 140 items that measures three dimensions of occupational stress: occupational stressors, personal strains and coping responses. An important feature of the OSI is that norm data are available, so that information from one group of employees can be compared to what would be expected for this group based on stress levels in other organizations.

This chapter has presented methods of evaluating the effectiveness of interventions for occupational stress. These methods can also serve other functions, such as measuring climate, and these have been highlighted. We close this chapter by providing an example of programme evaluation within a particular company (Exhibit 7.1).

Exhibit 7.1

Evaluation in the Work World

Paul Dyer

Goals for Evaluation

When occupational stress is too high, widespread and exists for prolonged periods, it has numerous deleterious consequences for the organization. The proper use of measurement is a necessary ingredient and a major challenge for any organization concerned about monitoring and regulating organizational stress. At least four important goals exist for measuring and understanding stress: to understand the organization's degree or level of stress; to identify sources of stress; to develop ways to track changes in stress over time; and to measure stress within smaller subsets of the total population.

Technical Quality

In addition to these four goals, researchers must also be concerned about the technical quality of the evaluation. This is because it makes little sense to ask an organization to change direction and commit dollars and other resources based on data that have limited accuracy and/or that do not suggest directions for change. Time, political issues, funding and other resource matters often make conducting quality applied evaluation research extremely difficult. However, those doing organizational research should not compromise on technical soundness. It is better not to measure than to do so poorly. Contrary to a widespread belief, 'some data' are not necessarily better than 'no data'. Some bad data are much worse than no data, since without data, decision makers often rely upon their 'gut'. Gut decisions based on years of experience and philosophical inquiry and analysis are much more likely to be effective than decisions based on inaccurate numbers.

How to Accomplish Evaluation Research

The next paragraph briefly outlines one approach to accomplish these four objectives and to ensure technical quality. This outline assumes that an organization is already regularly conducting employee opinion surveys. If this is not the case, an organization could either begin an employee survey process, or conduct a 'mini' survey that deals with occupational stress only.

As a first step, search the organizational behaviour and industrial psychology literature for publications regarding occupational stress. Numerous articles report statistically sound scales that measure various components of occupational stress such as role ambiguity and overload. Secondly, customize the items if necessary to fit in with your culture, pilot the scales in your own organization and then recalculate scale statistics. If technical expertise for scaling does not exist in your organization, either contact an industrial psychologist consultant or academician, or use the scale as published. Thirdly, incorporate the scales into the body of your employee opinion survey. To really understand occupational stress within your organization, you will need to understand it within the broader context of employee opinions about other issues such as supervision, participation, performance evaluation, and so on. Because the scales can easily be extracted from the survey and used independently, they are quite useful for assessing a work group or other subset of the entire organization. This is often a good first step in organizational development projects.

How to Accomplish Change

As a last point, even if measurement is done well, it may add little value to the organization. The entire change process must be considered. It is absolutely critical to define the stakeholders, understand their goals, gain their interest and involvement, and design a process for how the stakeholders will use the data to bring about positive change; all of these things should be accomplished prior to collecting data. Far too many times both good and poor quality 'real world' research suffers the same fate: it is put on hold, studied further, denied, rationalized, and so on. In short, very interesting but . . . so what. For measurement to be useful in improving organizational effectiveness, it must be seen as one part of a larger process of changing an organization and not seen as an end in itself.

Paul Dyer, an industrial psychologist, works for Dow Chemical Company, headquartered in Midland, Michigan.

8
Sample Materials

Throughout this book, an effort has been made to offer practical suggestions for how human resource management practitioners can intervene to help workers deal with occupational stress. Models for conceptualizing the kinds of interventions that would be most useful for coping with various kinds of stressors have been offered. In addition, strategies for implementing these interventions have been presented. In this final chapter, we offer sample materials to be used in conjunction with some of the coping strategies presented throughout this book. The materials are grouped into three sections: general stress management (handouts 1 to 8); assertiveness and communication (handouts 9 to 18); and relaxation and exercise (handouts 19 to 25).

General Stress Management Materials

The materials included in this section focus on the general topic of stress management. These materials would be useful as outlines or handouts to introduce workers to the topics of stress and stress management. In particular, the practitioner might use these materials in designing a stress management workshop (for example, a lunch-time series on stress topics). Similarly, these materials could be used as background material in publishing written material or producing tapes on stress.

Handouts 1 and 8 are general fact sheets on stress. Handouts 2 to 7 are inventories that can be used to help employees identify stress symptoms and stressful events.

DEFINITIONS

Handout 1

The following definitions will be helpful to you as you begin to learn about how you might best cope with stress in your life.

Stress:
- Bodily reaction to some stimuli in the environment.

Anxiety:
- Learned. Pairing of stimuli and response.
- Emotional response to a threatening situation or object.
- Prepares body for fight or flight.
- Normal reaction to stresses of life; no one is anxiety free.
- Can be useful to us by causing increased alertness, taking important things seriously, and motivating change and development.

Distress:
- Unmanaged stress and anxiety.
- Anxiety is a problem when it occurs in response to non-threatening stimuli or events and/or is an unrealistic fear of failing at tasks.

Possible consequences of distress:
- Impaired health.
- Blood pressure increases in response to stress.
- Increased blood pressure can increase incidence of hardening of arteries, hcart attacks and strokes.
- Combined with other factors, such as heredity, diet and exercise, high blood pressure and associated disorders account for almost half of all deaths in the United States and the United Kingdom.

STRESSFUL EVENTS INVENTORY

Handout 2

If you have experienced any of the following events during the past year, write the point value for that item in the points column. Add up your points to get your score

Life stress measure

	Life event	Point value	Points
1	Death of spouse	100	____
2	Divorce	73	____
3	Marital separation	65	____
4	Jail term	63	____
5	Death of close family member	63	____
6	Personal injury or illness	53	____
7	Marriage	50	____
8	Fired at work	47	____
9	Marital reconciliation	45	____
10	Retirement	45	____
11	Change in health of family member	44	____
12	Pregnancy	40	____
13	Sex difficulties	39	____
14	Gain of new family member	39	____
15	Business readjustment	39	____
16	Change in financial state	38	____
17	Death of a close friend	37	____
18	Change to different line of work	36	____
19	Change in number of arguments with spouse	35	____
20	Large loan/mortgage	31	____
21	Foreclosure of mortgage or loan	30	____
22	Change in responsibilities at work	29	____
23	Son or daughter leaving home	29	____
24	Trouble with in-laws	29	____
25	Outstanding personal achievement	28	____
26	Spouse begins or stops work	26	____
27	Begin or end school	26	____
28	Change in living conditions	25	____
29	Revision of personal habits	24	____
30	Trouble with boss	23	____
31	Change in work hours or conditions	20	____
32	Change in residence	20	____
33	Change in schools	20	____

Handout 2 *cont.*

Life stress measure

	Life event	Point value	Points
34	Change in recreation	19	___
35	Change in church activities	19	___
36	Change in social activities	18	___
37	Minor loan/mortgage	17	___
38	Change in sleeping habits	16	___
39	Change in number of family get-togethers	15	___
40	Change in eating habits	15	___
41	Vacation	13	___
42	Christmas	12	___
43	Minor violations of the law	11	___
		Total	___

STRESS SYMPTOM INVENTORY

Handout 3

The following lists are common problems associated with too much stress. Mark the frequency with which you have experienced each of these problems during the past two months with the following symbols:

X – haven't had this problem
O – occasionally
F – frequently
C – constant or nearly constant occurrence

Physical	*Emotional*	*Spiritual*
__overeating	__anxiety	__emptiness
__tension headaches	__frustration	__loss of meaning
__migraine headaches	__the 'blues'	__doubt
__tension	__mood swings	__unforgiving
__fatigue	__bad temper	__martyrdom
__insomnia	__nightmares	__looking for magic
__weight change	__crying spells	__loss of direction
__colds	__irritability	__needing to prove self
__muscle aches	__'no one cares'	__cynicism
__constipation	__depression	__apathy
__pounding heart	__nervous laugh	
__accident prone	__worrying	
__early morning awakening	__easily discouraged	
__teeth grinding	__little joy	
__rash		
__nervousness		
__foot-tapping		
__finger drumming		
__increased alcohol, drug, tobacco use		
__menstrual distress		
__high blood pressure		
__indigestion		
__low-grade infections		
__cold hands and feet		

Handout 3 *cont.*

Mental	*Relational*
__forgetfulness	__isolation
__dull senses	__intolerance
__poor concentration	__resentment
__low productivity	__loneliness
__confusion	__lashing out
__lethargy	__hiding
__whirling mind	__clamming up
__no new ideas	__nagging
__boredom	__distrust
__spacing out	__fewer contacts with friends
__negative self talk	__lack of intimacy
__not enjoying self often	__comments from others that you seem tense
	__using people

Adapted from *Structured Exercises in Stress Management Vol. I.* Nancy Louing Tubesing and Donald A. Tubesing, Editors, Whole Person Press, 1983.

DISTRESS SYMPTOMS OR SIGNALS

Handout 4

As a way to begin to evaluate how much distress you are experiencing in your life, consider the list of symptoms below. Place a tick next to all the symptoms that describe you currently.

____Expression of boredom with much or everything.
____Tendency to begin vacillating in decision making.
____Tendency to become distraught with trifles.
____Inattentiveness or loss of power to concentrate.
____Irritability.
____Procrastination.
____Feelings of persecution.
____Gut-level feelings of unexplainable dissatisfaction.
____Forgetfulness.
____Tendency to misjudge people.
____Uncertain about whom to trust.
____Inability to organize self.
____Inner confusion about duties or roles.
____Physical changes such as:
    ____Sudden, noticeable loss or gain of weight
    ____Sudden change of appearance
    ____Decline or improvement in dress
    ____Sudden changes of complexion (sallow, reddened, acne)
    ____Difficult breathing
    ____Sudden change in smoking habits
    ____Sudden change in use of alcohol
    ____Allergies or new allergies
    ____Sudden facial expression changes
    ____Sudden changes in social habits
    ____Not going to work or home according to past schedule
    ____Change of life situation or style (for example, marriage, birth of baby, divorce, death of spouse)

STRESS DANGER SIGNALS

Handout 5

There are certain signs common to stress. Medical measures of stress can be determined by a physician, but there are many signs that you can observe yourself.

1 General irritability, hyperexcitation, or depression.
2 Pounding of the heart.
3 Dryness of throat and mouth.
4 Impulsive behaviour.
5 The overpowering urge to cry or run and hide.
6 Inability to concentrate, flight of thoughts and general disorientation.
7 Feelings of unreality, weakness, or dizziness.
8 Fatigue.
9 Floating anxiety, being afraid and not knowing why.
10 Emotional tension and alertness – keyed up.
11 Trembling, nervous tics.
12 Tendency to be easily startled by small sounds.
13 High-pitched, nervous laughter.
14 Stuttering and other speech difficulties.
15 Bruxism, or grinding of the teeth.
16 Insomnia.
17 Hypermobility, an increased tendency to move about without any reason.
18 Sweating.
19 The frequent need to urinate.
20 Diarrhoea, indigestion, queasiness in the stomach and sometimes vomiting.
21 Migraine headaches.
22 Premenstrual tension or missed menstrual cycles.
23 Pain in the neck or lower back.
24 Loss of or excessive appetite.
25 Increased smoking.
26 Increased use of legally prescribed drugs.
27 Nightmares.
28 Neurotic behaviour.
29 Psychoses.
30 Accident proneness.

From *The Stress of Life* by Hans Selye. Copyright 1978 by McGraw-Hill Book Company, New York. Used with permission of McGraw-Hill Book Company.

HOW VULNERABLE ARE YOU TO STRESS?

Handout 6

The following test was developed by psychologists Lyle H. Miller and Alma Dell Smith at the Boston University Medical Center. Score each item from 1 (almost always) to 5 (never), according to how much of the time each statement applies to you.

1 I eat at least one hot, balanced meal a day.
2 I get seven to eight hours sleep at least four nights a week.
3 I give and receive affection regularly.
4 I have at least one relative within 50 miles on whom I can rely.
5 I exercise to the point of perspiration at least twice a week.
6 I smoke less than half a pack of cigarettes a day.
7 I take fewer than five alcoholic drinks a week.
8 I am the appropriate weight for my height.
9 I have an income adequate to meet basic expenses.
10 I get strength from my religious beliefs.
11 I regularly attend club or social activities.
12 I have a network of friends and acquaintances.
13 I have one or more friends to confide in about personal matters.
14 I am in good health (including eyesight, hearing, teeth).
15 I am able to speak openly about my feelings when angry or worried.
16 I have regular conversations with the people I live with about domestic problems (for example, chores, money and daily living issues).
17 I do something for fun at least once a week.
18 I am able to organize my time effectively.
19 I drink fewer than three cups of coffee (or tea or cola drinks) a day.
20 I take quiet time for myself during the day.

TOTAL____

To obtain your score, add up the figures and subtract 20. Any number over 30 indicates a vulnerability to stress. You are seriously vulnerable if your score is between 50 and 75, and extremely vulnerable if it is over 75.

STRESSFUL ATTITUDES ASSESSMENT

Handout 7

This test assesses how you are feeling about your life. Study the following statements and circle the answer that best applies to you.

Attitude or feeling	How often feeling occurs			
	Almost never	Occasionally	Frequently	Almost always
1 Things must be perfect.	1	2	3	4
2 I must do it myself.	1	2	3	4
3 I feel more isolated from my family or close friends.	1	2	3	4
4 I feel that people should listen better.	1	2	3	4
5 My life is running me.	1	2	3	4
6 I must not fail.	1	2	3	4
7 When overworked, I cannot say no to new demands without feeling guilty.	1	2	3	4
8 I need to generate excitement again and again to avoid boredom.	1	2	3	4
9 I feel a lack of intimacy with people around me.	1	2	3	4
10 I am unable to relax.	1	2	3	4
11 I feel increasingly cynical and disenchanted.	1	2	3	4
12 I am unable to laugh at a joke about myself.	1	2	3	4
13 I avoid speaking my mind.	1	2	3	4
14 I feel under pressure to succeed all the time.	1	2	3	4
15 I automatically express negative attitudes.	1	2	3	4
16 I seem further behind at the end of the day than when I started.	1	2	3	4
17 I forget deadlines, appointments and personal possessions.	1	2	3	4

Handout 7 *cont.*

Attitude or feeling	How often feeling occurs			
	Almost never	Occasion-ally	Fre-quently	Almost always
18 I am irritable, short-tempered, disappointed in the people around me.	1	2	3	4
19 Sex seems like more trouble than it's worth.	1	2	3	4
20 I consider myself exploited.	1	2	3	4
21 I wake up earlier and cannot sleep.	1	2	3	4
22 I feel unrested.	1	2	3	4
23 I feel dissatisfied with my work life.	1	2	3	4
24 I feel dissatisfied with my personal life.	1	2	3	4
25 I'm not where I want to be in life.	1	2	3	4
26 I avoid being alone.	1	2	3	4
27 I have trouble getting to sleep.	1	2	3	4
28 I have trouble waking up.	1	2	3	4
29 I can't seem to get out of bed.	1	2	3	4

Score yourself: 29 and below = low stress; 30 to 50 = mild stress; 59 to 87 = moderate stress; 88 to 116 = high stress

THE AAAbc's OF STRESS MANAGEMENT

Handout 8

The AAAbc's of stress management is based on ideas presented by Joe E. Dunlap and J. Douglas Stewart in *Keeping the Fire Alive*. Tulsa: Penwell, 1983.

Highlights:

- Stress management is a decision making process. Three major ways to deal with stress are to:
  <u>A</u>lter it
  <u>A</u>void it
  <u>A</u>ccept it by
      <u>b</u>uilding our resistance or
      <u>c</u>hanging our perception

- Different situations will determine the appropriate approach.

- <u>A</u>ltering implies removing the source of stress by changing something.
  problem solving
  direct communication
  organization
  planning
  time management

- <u>A</u>voiding implies removing oneself from the stressful situation or figuring out how not to get there in the first place.
  walk away
  let go
  say 'no'
  delegate
  know limits

- <u>A</u>ccepting involves equipping oneself physically and mentally for stress by <u>b</u>uilding resistance and <u>c</u>hanging the way we perceive things.
  building resistance –
      proper diet; regular aerobic exercise; relaxation techniques; positive affirmation; taking time for oneself; getting clear about goals, priorities, values; building and maintaining support systems; investing in relationships; clear communication; intimacy; meditation.

  changing the way you perceive the situation or yourself – unrealistic expectations; irrational beliefs.

Assertiveness and Communication Skills

Some of the interventions described in the previous chapters included reference to the importance of being assertive in coping with stressful situations in the workplace. The materials in this section are designed to be used as part of a stress management intervention to teach individuals better communication skills as a means of coping with occupational stress. Handout 9 offers a sample agenda for an assertiveness training programme. Supporting materials for this programme are included in handouts 10–18.

SAMPLE AGENDA FOR ASSERTIVENESS TRAINING PROGRAMME

Handout 9

The agenda outlined below describes some of the major components that have been covered in assertiveness training programmes (for a more complete review, see Chapter 5). These sessions have been designed to allow a practitioner to teach these skills in short segments (for example, over lunch; during breaks) which often fits better with an employee's schedule. In addition, having time between sessions allows employees to practise the skills and even 'troubleshoot' problems that have arisen. The practitioner should note that this same agenda could be used with an individual employee or group. In fact, some success has been seen in groups as members are able to share experiences and offer support as they learn new skills.

Session	Topics to be covered
1	• Introduce overview of course. • Describe/distinguish between communication styles: passive, aggressive, and assertive. • Introduce assertiveness inventory.
2	• Introduce behaviour change contract. • Discuss developing an assertive stance. • Introduce interpersonal rights and rational belief systems.
3	• Describe steps in being assertive. • Allow participants to role play. • Assign homework to practise being assertive.
4	• Troubleshoot problems with homework assignments. • Discuss strategies for difficult interpersonal situations: requesting help, protesting habits, saying 'no', dealing with the 'silent treatment', reacting to unjust criticism.

ASSERTIVENESS TRAINING REGISTRATION FORM

Handout 10

Your responses on this form are confidential and will be used by the facilitator to tailor the programme to meet your needs.

Name:

What brought you to this group?

What do you want to focus on in this group?

Any past experiences with assertiveness or communication styles? If so, what?

Write down the first word that comes to mind when you hear the word 'assertive':

What are your expectations of your group experience?

Is there a particular manner in which you learn best (discussion, reading, lectures, etc.)?

List one (or more) thing(s) you really like about yourself:

What are your hobbies and interests?

Handout 11

DISTINGUISHING BETWEEN COMMUNICATION STYLES

	Non-assertive	Assertive	Aggressive
Behaviours	Inaction Sacrificing Apologizing Whining Giving in Demanding in a subtle way Unwilling to compromise	Calm persistence Forthright stating of opinions Open stating of desires Calm pursuance of reasonable goals Admitting mistakes and flaws Sense of humour Willing to compromise	Shouting Slamming doors, drawers, etc. Abusive language Name-calling Threats–verbal, physical Demanding in overt way Unwilling to compromise
Feelings	Fear Anxiety Guilt Depression Resentment Hostility	Calm, relaxed Mild, negative feelings such as irritation annoyance regret sadness concern	Anger Anxiety Hostility Depression Fear Often leads to guilt
Non-verbal cues	Soft voice Stuttering Stooped, withdrawn Little or no eye contact Nervous gestures	Moderate voice Moderate speech pace Upright posture Appropriate eye contact Appropriate gestures	Loud voice Rapid-fire speech pace 'Attack' stance Staring 'Attack' gestures

Handout 11 *cont.*

	Non-assertive	Assertive	Aggressive
Thoughts	I can't do it. I shouldn't do it.	This is new to me, but I can try. Others may disapprove, but I can live with that.	I'm right; they're wrong. They should do what I want.
	I should do it.	It would be best for me to do it.	I have to get my way, no matter what.
	I have to do it.	I'm neither worthwhile nor worthless, but a fallible human being.	I'm wonderful; they're rotten.
	They're making me do it. They're right, I'm wrong. I can't get what I want.	I may or may not get what I want, but I'll try.	I can't get what I want and that's terrible.

ASSERTIVENESS INVENTORY

Handout 12

Read each of the situations below. For each item, make a rating of whether the situation represents a problem/difficulty for you. Use the following scale in making your rating:

1 = never a problem
2 = occasionally a problem
3 = a problem about half the time
4 = often a problem
5 = always a problem

	never				always
1 Turn down a request to borrow money.	1	2	3	4	5
2 Compliment a friend or co-worker.	1	2	3	4	5
3 Receive compliments.	1	2	3	4	5
4 Ask a favour of someone that will mean time/work/effort for him/her.	1	2	3	4	5
5 Resist sales pressure from clerks who try to sell you merchandise you don't want.	1	2	3	4	5
6 Apologize when you know you've done something wrong.	1	2	3	4	5
7 Return merchandise.	1	2	3	4	5
8 In a close relationship, tell the other when he or she says something that upsets you.	1	2	3	4	5
9 Start a conversation with a stranger or new acquaintance.	1	2	3	4	5
10 Admit 'I don't know' when you're ignorant about something.	1	2	3	4	5
11 Ask personal questions.	1	2	3	4	5
12 Answer personal questions.	1	2	3	4	5
13 Apply for a job.	1	2	3	4	5
14 Ask for a raise.	1	2	3	4	5
15 Delegate authority to a woman.	1	2	3	4	5
16 Delegate authority to a man.	1	2	3	4	5
17 Quit a job you don't like.	1	2	3	4	5
18 Say no when someone makes a completely unfair demand of you.	1	2	3	4	5

Handout 12 *cont.*

	never				always
19 Tell someone 'I like what you did'.	1	2	3	4	5
20 Tell someone 'I don't like what you did'.	1	2	3	4	5
21 Get off the telephone with a long-winded friend.	1	2	3	4	5
22 Make social overtures (dates, dinner) to a female, a couple, a male.	1	2	3	4	5
23 Answer a hostile, unjustified put-down.	1	2	3	4	5
24 Discuss a justified criticism of your behaviour with the other person.	1	2	3	4	5
25 Refuse a date when you don't like the person.	1	2	3	4	5
26 End a relationship which has become unsatisfactory.	1	2	3	4	5
27 Resist sexual advances when you have no interest.	1	2	3	4	5
28 Ask for a better table in a restaurant when the host/hostess puts you and a friend next to the kitchen.	1	2	3	4	5
29 Send back food in a restaurant when it arrives and isn't what you've ordered.	1	2	3	4	5
30 Stand up for yourself when your mother/father-in-law attacks you.	1	2	3	4	5
31 Request the return of borrowed items.	1	2	3	4	5
32 Say something when another person takes credit for your work.	1	2	3	4	5
33 Tell another person when he/she has done something that has offended you.	1	2	3	4	5
34 Tell good news about yourself to: friends, family, husband/wife/partner.	1	2	3	4	5

Handout 12 *cont.*

		never				always
35	If single, be able to go out with a couple and no partner for you.	1	2	3	4	5
36	Go alone to a party.	1	2	3	4	5
37	Tell a person – whether boss, lover, spouse, friend – when he/she has done something wrong in a professional sense.	1	2	3	4	5
38	Speak up at a meeting.	1	2	3	4	5
39	Feel you have the right to choose your own lifestyle even though others may disagree with it.	1	2	3	4	5
40	Say 'I love you' aloud and mean it.	1	2	3	4	5
41	Express a sexual want to your partner.	1	2	3	4	5

DEVELOPING AN ASSERTIVE STANCE

Handout 13

What can a person observe about his or her own behaviour which will indicate whether he or she is being assertive? Here are a few simple components which go together to constitute an assertive act:

Non-verbal

1 Eye contact: Looking directly at another person when one is speaking is an effective way of declaring that one is sincere about what one is saying, and that it is directed to that person.
2 Body posture: The 'weight' of one's message to others will be increased if you face the person, stand or sit appropriately close, lean towards him or her, hold your head erect.
3 Gestures: A message accented with appropriate gestures takes on an added emphasis (overenthusiastic gesturing can be distracting).
4 Facial expression: Effective assertions require an expression that agrees with the message (don't express anger while smiling).
5 Voice tone, inflection, volume: A whispered monotone will seldom convince another person that one means business, while a shouted epithet will bring down defenses into the path of communication. A level, well-modulated conversational statement is convincing without being intimidating.
6 Timing: Spontaneous expression will generally be one's goal, since hesitation may diminish the effect of an assertion. Judgement is necessary, however, to select an appropriate occasion in which to confront another person or to discuss personal matters.

Verbal

7 Content: Although what one says is important, it is often less important than most believe. A fundamental honesty in interpersonal communication and spontaneity of expression are encouraged. That means, for example, forcefully, 'I'm damn mad at what you did!' rather than, 'You're an S.O.B!' People who have for years hesitated because they 'didn't know *what* to say' find that the practice of saying something to express their feelings at the time is a valuable step towards greater spontaneous assertiveness.
8 Use of 'I' statements: It is important to take responsibility or 'to own' what you are feeling or thinking.

DISTINGUISHING BETWEEN VERBAL AND NON-VERBAL COMMUNICATION

Handout 14

Non-assertive	Assertive	Aggressive
Verbal aspects of communication		
Statements that imply 'I don't care' or 'I'm not important'.	Statements that reflect your feelings of self-worth and self-respect.	Defensive, superior statements or comments that put down the capabilities of others.
All-or-nothing thinking. If you don't have a skill or capability totally, then you can't give yourself *any* credit.	Realistic assessment and honest expression of your capabilities.	Overblown description of what you can do and defensive response to any questioning of your qualifications.
Minimization of your skills and accomplishments by much use of qualifiers such as 'sort of'.	Appropriate use of adjectives and adverbs to indicate your motivation and enthusiasm.	Insincere or overplayed description of your accomplishments.
Hope that others will be able to infer your skills and abilities from your general statements.	Specific, concise statements of your skills and abilities illustrated by your accomplishments and achievements.	Exaggerated and misleading statements of your skills and capabilities.

Handout 14 *cont.*

Non-assertive	Assertive	Aggressive
Non-verbal aspects of communication		
Even if verbal message is assertive, non-verbal behaviour implies that you don't believe what you say.	Non-verbal behaviour is congruent with the verbal message.	Non-verbal behaviour is demanding, cocky and hostile.
Communicates indecisiveness self-effacement and anxiety.	Communicates self-assurance, comfort and attentiveness.	Communicates competiveness lack of respect and superiority.
Speech may be awkward, hesitant and filled with pauses and nervous laughter. Mouth is dry and throat is cleared frequently.	Speech is fluent, expressive and concise. Voice is appropriately loud, firm and relaxed.	Speech may be rapid, loud and tense. Tone seems to be condescending, defensive or challenging. Voice may be cold or shrill.
Eye contact is largely absent.	Eye contact is direct, but not staring.	Eye contact is overly frank, staring, or seems to look through the other person.
Gestures are distracting, wooden, self-deprecating. Tend to soften the impact of your statements.	Gestures are appropriate and relaxed. Serve to add support and emphasis to what you're saying.	Gestures are abrupt, rigid and intrusive. Others may feel overwhelmed or attacked.

SAMPLE BEHAVIOUR CHANGE CONTRACT

Handout 15

Assertiveness Training
Behaviour Change Contract

Name _____   Date _____

After completing the assertiveness inventory, please complete the items below:

1   Describe the area of behaviour on which you would like to focus.

2   Identify when and under what conditions this problem behaviour situation occurs.

3   List concepts and ideas from the training programme that might help you deal with the situation you have identified.

4   Outline specific behaviour changes you would like to see.

5   Identify the exercises that were outlined in training that will help you make the behaviour change.

6   Describe any roadblocks you anticipate.

LIST OF IRRATIONAL BELIEFS

Handout 16

Many people have preconceived ideas, thoughts or beliefs about the world that can make being assertive difficult. We need to move from focusing on irrational beliefs to more rational ones. Read the sample list of irrational beliefs below.

1   Irrational belief: If I assert myself, others will get mad at me.
   Rational belief: If I assert myself, the effects may be positive, neutral, or negative. The person may or may not get mad at me/they may feel closer to me/like what I say or do/help me to solve the problem. Since assertion involves legitimate rights, I feel that the odds are in my favour to have some positive results.

2   Irrational belief: If I assert myself and people do become angry with me, I will be devastated; it will be awful.
   Rational belief: Even if others do become angry and unpleasant, I am capable of handling it without falling apart. If I can assert myself when it is appropriate, I don't have to feel responsible for the other person's anger. It may be his problem.

3   Irrational belief: Although I prefer others to be straightforward with me, I'm afraid that if I am open with others and say 'no', I will hurt them.
   Rational belief: If I'm assertive, other people may or may not feel hurt. Most people are not more fragile than I am. If I prefer to be dealt with directly, quite likely others will too.

4   Irrational belief: If my assertion hurts others, I am responsible for their feelings.
   Rational belief: Even if others do feel hurt by my assertive behaviour, I can let them know I care for them while also being direct about what I need or want. Although at times others will be taken aback by my assertive behaviour, most people are not so vulnerable and fragile that they will be shattered by it.

5   Irrational belief: It is wrong and selfish to turn down legitimate requests. Other people will think I'm terrible and won't like me.
   Rational belief: Even legitimate requests can be refused assertively. Also, it is acceptable to consider my own needs – sometimes before those of others. And I can't please all of the people all of the time.

Handout 16 *cont.*

6   Irrational belief: At all costs, I must avoid making statements and asking questions that might make me look ignorant and stupid.
Rational belief: It's all right to lack information or to make a mistake. It just shows I'm human.

7   Irrational belief: Assertive women are cold, castrating bitches. If I'm assertive I'll be so unpleasant that people won't like me.
Rational belief: Assertive people are direct and honest, and behave appropriately. They show a genuine concern for other people's rights and feelings.

SPECIAL INTERPERSONAL SITUATIONS

Handout 17

The following tips or guidelines have been designed to help you cope with three different interpersonal situations in which people find it difficult to be assertive.

Refusing a request

1 Decide how legitimate the request is. Even if it is legitimate, you have a right to turn down a legitimate request once in a while.

2 Be aware of what your body tells you. If you feel uptight and tense, probably you are not wanting to grant the request.

3 Ask for more information before agreeing to do something you're not sure about.

4 Take some time to think it over, if necessary. Simply say, 'I'd like some time to think it over.' You are not required to give an answer on the spot in most cases, even if the other person thinks you are.

5 When saying no, be as brief as possible. One brief explanation is all that is necessary. The more you tend to run on, the weaker your excuses become and the better the other person's chances of getting you to change your mind.

6 Actually say the word 'no'. Not, 'Well, I really don't think I . . .' No is less ambiguous.

7 If necessary, repeat the original brief explanation once. This is called the 'broken-record technique'.

8 Make your non-verbals match your verbals. Shake your head no. Do not look or talk apologetically! Often people tend to smile when refusing a request.

9 Avoid the words 'I'm sorry'. Often this becomes a habit and is not genuinely meant.

10 Own it as your decision. Don't attribute it to others. Actively take the responsibility. Not: 'I can't' but: 'I won't' or 'I don't care to', etc.

Saying 'no'

1 Be as brief as possible, that is, give a legitimate reason for your refusal, 'I really don't have the time', and avoid long, elaborate explanations, justifications, and 'lies', such as 'I can't because my mother is arriving from out of town, and I still have a lot of errands to run, and I haven't finished my report yet, and my child is ill . . .', etc., etc.

Handout 17 *cont.*

2 Actually say the word 'no' when declining. The word 'no' has more power and is less ambiguous than, 'Well, I just don't think so . . .', 'I really can't just now . . .', etc.

3 Repetition and persistence may be necessary. You may have to decline several times before the person 'hears' you. It's not necessary to come up with a new explanation each time, you can use your original reason over and over again.

4 Shake your head when saying 'no'. Often people unknowingly nod their heads and smile when they are attempting to decline or refuse. Make sure your non-verbal gestures mirror your verbal messages.

5 Boycott the words 'I'm sorry'. Try to be conscious about using this phrase to excuse your refusal or otherwise weaken your credibility. Habitual use of this phrase can be distracting to your real intent.

Handling criticism (how to respond to criticism assertively)

1 If it's fair criticism, ask for specific suggestions, alternatives, from the person. What might you do to handle a situation, or behave differently?

2 No need for long, self-critical, or rationalizing excuses.

3 When a person's criticism is somewhat vague, unclear, for example, 'You are "cold" with people', have them clarify, give specific examples.

4 Respond with opinion statements rather than 'you' statements, for example, 'I think you misinterpreted what I said', instead of, 'Your interpretation is all wrong.'

5 It's OK to share your reactions, feelings, regarding the criticism: 'I feel a little angry about your bringing up this issue again', or 'I feel unjustly criticized.'

HOMEWORK ASSIGNMENT DISCUSSION SHEET

Handout 18

Use the following questions to assess how well you completed the assignments that included an attempt at being assertive.

1 Did you feel confident and good about the assertion you displayed?

2 Did you stand up for your rights without violating the rights of others?

    (a) What rights were you standing up for in the situation?

    (b) On a scale of 0–10, 10 being very confident, 0 being not confident, how much confidence did you feel in owning your rights in the situation?

3 Did you say and do what you wanted to say and do?

    (a) Did you speak directly, objectively, and non-apologetically, stating what you wanted?

    (b) Were your voice and body calm and firm?

4 Did you tell positive things as you were being assertive?

5 Were you aware of the consequences to yourself and to the other person of being assertive in the situation? Were you willing to face and/or act on those consequences?

Relaxation and Exercise

In Chapter 5 we discussed how individuals might use exercise and relaxation skills to buffer the effects of stress. In Chapter 6, we described the health and well-being programmes that organizations are using to help employees deal with stress. The final section in this chapter contains material that a practitioner might find useful in introducing employees to exercise and relaxation as a means of coping with stress. There are far too many materials written on this topic to include them all here. Instead, these samples should serve as an introduction to the kinds of materials that can be used. Handout 19 includes a sample agenda a practitioner could use in designing a relaxation training programme. Handouts 20–24 contain general information about relaxation together with instructions in how to do specific relaxation techniques. Handouts 24 and 25 focus on information about choosing a recreation/ exercise programme.

SUGGESTED AGENDA FOR RELAXATION TRAINING

Handout 19

Session	Topics to be covered
1	Introduction to course.
	Discuss the relaxation response.
	Teach breathing techniques.
2	Review homework
	Review quick techniques for relaxation.
	Introduce progressive muscle relaxation (PMR).
	Assign PMR practice.
3	Review progress on PMR.
	Introduce guided imagery.
	Assign continued PMR practice.
4	Review progress on PMR.
	Conduct guided imagery exercise.
	Assign guided imagery practice.
5	Review progress on guided imagery exercises.
	Discuss other uses of guided imagery.
	Assign continued practice.
6	Review course content.
	Discuss exercise and overall 'wellness' plan.
	Introduce personal action plan and allow participants to create their plan.
	Evaluate the course.

ELEMENTS OF THE RELAXATION RESPONSE

Handout 20

Relaxation is a form of meditation – a state of concentration. By using the mind to focus upon an object, image, or thought, one cancels out all distraction associated with everyday life. The 'Relaxation Response' is induced to counterbalance the stress response.

There are four basic elements of the 'Relaxation Response':

1   A quiet environment – to turn off external distractions.
2   A comfortable position – sitting or kneeling with back straight – no tight clothing.
3   An object, thought, or image to dwell upon (repetition of a word or sound such as 'one', focusing upon breathing, or saying, 'I am relaxed').
4   A passive attitude – allowing an emptying of distracting thoughts.

Relaxation *is not*:

1   A loss of control.
2   A loss of consciousness.
3   A state of sleep.
4   A state of drowsiness.

With regular practice once or twice a day for 10–15 minutes, the following results are possible:

During relaxation you will experience:

1   A decrease in the rate of metabolism, a restful state with a drop in heart rate and respiratory rate.
2   A marked decrease in the body's oxygen consumption.
3   A decrease in blood pressure.
4   A decrease in muscle tension.

After relaxation, you may notice carry over effects including:

1   Lower response to stress – less anxiety.
2   Better coping abilities.
3   A new found acceptance of self, more tolerant of own weaknesses or limitations.
4   Improved learning ability, better retention and recall.
5   A sense of calm, of being collected – a more quiet, philosophical attitude.

TECHNIQUES

Handout 21

In order to help obtain the best possible results it is good to do your relaxation exercises in quiet surroundings where you will have few distractions. Besides this there are some other things you can do to make relaxing easier. The following list shows you some of these.

1 Plan regular times for relaxing in your day. Try to pick two, 20 minute periods where you have nothing else planned. This is your time. Don't try to force yourself to relax when you have other things that must be done.
2 Practice on an empty stomach if you can. Never practice after you eat.
3 Sometimes when you first relax thoughts or feelings will come to mind that cause you to be more tense. These thoughts can be controlled with practice so you can relax.
4 Don't use relaxation exercises as a substitute for medical advice. If you have a medical problem please let your doctor know you are practising relaxation.
5 If you have contact lenses in your eyes, they should be removed before relaxation therapy begins. Leaving them in can cause pain due to increased tear production as well as inability to concentrate due to the feeling of the contact lenses in your eyes.
6 When relaxing find a comfortable sitting or lying position. Loosen tight clothing and take off your shoes. If you are cold cover yourself with a lightweight blanket. The following are positions that are best for relaxing.

Sitting
Use a comfortable but supportive chair. Sit with your back straight, your head forward with your knees bent at 90 degree angles. Let your arms rest comfortably on top of your legs. If you feel tightness in any muscles shift your position until you are more at ease.

Lying
Lie flat with your arms slightly away from your body. Place your hands palm down with fingers spread so they aren't touching. Bend your elbows slightly away from your body. You can use small pillows to support your neck, knees and arms if needed.

When finished with the exercises, stretch your arms and legs and count from one to five slowly to give yourself time to become more alert.

SHORT TECHNIQUES FOR QUICK RELAXATION

Handout 22

Head rolls
Roll head in circle, 2–3 times to right, then 2–3 times to the left. Do rolls slowly, not forcing head if muscles feel stiff. Do as often as needed.

Shoulder rolls
Raise shoulders as if you were a puppet. Move shoulders in a circle, then drop and relax them as circle is completed. Do circle in either direction, whichever feels more relaxing. This can be done from any position. Good for relaxing while in the car or at work.

Toe raises
While standing, raise up on toes, tensing leg muscles. Hold for 3–5 seconds. Lower self to flat foot position, allowing muscles to relax. Bend knees slightly bouncing, letting tension leave legs and back. Good for relaxing while standing for long periods of time.

Muscle tension inventory
Take some time during your busy day to check the amount of tension you are holding in your muscles.

- Take a slow deep breath.
- As you exhale, pay attention to the different muscle groups, starting at your head and working down to your feet, letting any tension go as you do so.
- Feel a wave of relaxation throughout your body.
- Take one more deep breath and go on with your day.

Jaw drop
With your eyes open, let your jaw drop as if you were going to yawn. Let your tongue rest limply on the bottom of your mouth behind your teeth. Breathe slowly and rhythmically through your mouth and let yourself relax. This exercise takes about 10 minutes, and can be done while sitting at your desk, driving, walking, or doing work at home.

Relaxation bar
With your eyes closed, imagine a horizontal bar above your head. 'Watch' it slowly cross your body, from head to toe, and feel it bring relaxation to each part of the body that it crosses over. In this way, you are relaxing your head, neck, shoulders, chest, etc. As the bar reaches your toes, relaxation is felt throughout the body.

Handout 22   *cont.*

Word repetition
With eyes closed, silently repeat a relaxing word to yourself. At the same time, breathe in deeply drawing relaxation. On the second, breathe out the tension.

Sleep
When retiring to bed, lay upon the pillow while imagining and 'feeling' yourself sinking down into the bed.

Practical preparation for sleep
Here are some suggestions that may help you go to sleep more easily.

1   Choose quiet activities for the last few hours before you go to bed.
2   Try not to talk about hard-to-resolve problems before bedtime.
3   If the next day will be busy, plan for it early in the evening, and then move on to other things.
4   Don't go to bed until you are tired.
5   Plan regular exercise each day.
6   Take time to relax.
     (a) Take a warm bath.
     (b) Do a relaxation exercise.
     (c) Read.
     (d) Listen to quiet music.
7   Lie in a comfortable position in bed. Second, clear your mind by counting backward from 100.

BREATHING TECHNIQUES

Handout 23

The following exercises will be useful as you attempt to use deep breathing as a way to relax.

Cool air in, warm air out

1 Close eyes, sit in comfortable position.
2 Breathe in, concentrating on the air coming in through your nostrils.
3 Breathe out, concentrating on the air moving out.
4 Notice the air coming in seems to be cooler than the air going out.
5 Think of air coming in as being fresh and pure, and the air going out as sweeping out with it all your tensions and worries, which makes the air warm.

Abdominal breathing

1 Sit in chair keeping back straight (good posture).
2 Put one hand on your chest, and the other on your navel.
3 Breathe in and out, focusing on moving only your lower hand. Abdominal breathing encourages relaxation. Use this type of breathing for all breathing exercises.

Breathing for stressful situations

1 Remove yourself from situation – step to side or out of room.
2 Breathe in deeply for a count of 8.
3 As you exhale for count of 8, visualize yourself as being calm, relaxed, and in control.
4 Repeat sequence several times until level of relaxation is obtained.

Breathing to aid sleep

1 Assume desired sleeping position.
2 Focus on breathing.
3 While breathing out, focus on relaxing.
4 For first 2–3 exhalations, focus on the feeling of your body against the bed.
5 Continue breathing focusing on relaxing, letting all muscles go limp, noting the sinking and slowing down sensations.
6 Once totally relaxed, visualize breath as coloured vapour and see the air flow into and out of the body.
7 Continue focusing on breathing and relaxed feeling.
8 Sleep should result naturally.

Handout 23 *cont.*

Breathing for relaxation while at work or in car

1 If radio is available, turn station to soft, slow music.
2 Concentrate on beat of music, slow and steady.
3 Breathe in rhythm with music, focus on relaxing muscles during exhalation.
4 Or, if music is not available, follow instructions for 'Breathing for stressful situations'.

Breathing rhythmically with relaxation

1 Lay in comfortable position in darkened room.
2 Breathe in and out deeply through open mouth for count of 16. (8 counts in – 8 counts out).
3 Close eyes and focus yourself floating on air mattress on lake or pool.
4 Feel gentle wave motion of water.
5 Continue breathing, allowing body to become limp.
6 Picture lungs as a balloon, expanding and contracting with each breath movement.
7 Continue with sequence until complete relaxation is achieved.

When ready to end exercise

1 Breathe deeply, and move lower body with exhalation.
2 Breathe deeply again, and move upper body with exhalation.
3 With third deep breath open eyes and stretch muscles in body.

SUGGESTED RECREATION ACTIVITIES TO BALANCE DIFFERENT WORK SITUATIONS

Handout 24

It is important for individuals to have balance across activities in their life. Many people have found that if their work situation leads to one particular kind of stress they can balance their life by choosing recreational activities that differ from their work. Read the list below to determine which activities fit best for you.

If your work is:	You might benefit from:	You should consider:
You feel regimented, with little control over your life.	a chance to be in command. Perhaps team games are not for you. You should engage in activities for which you have laid out the time and rules.	photography, collecting (seashells, stamps, what have you), playing a musical instrument? For something more active try walking, roller skating, swimming.
Your personal life is full of tension and exasperation.	in addition to relaxation find some way to blow off steam. Avoid frustrating 'fun' and pursue some pastimes that are aggressively physical.	tennis, touch football, throwing darts, hitting a punching bag? Chopping wood can vent a lot of aggressive feelings. Yoga is great, or go and fly a kite.
Your work shows nothing tangible for your efforts.	the pleasure of making something from start to finish – preferably something that keeps, which you	ceramics, sewing and other fabric arts, making jewellery, working with metal or wood.

Handout 24 *cont.*

If your work is:	You might benefit from:	You should consider:
	can wear, hang on the wall or present to a friend.	If you don't mind having results disappear, try gourmet cooking.
Your work offers you no opportunity to be creative.	a means of self-expression. We all have some creativity within; experiment until you have found the way to tap yours.	painting, sketching, sculpting. Photography, home decorating, landscaping, garden, growing and arranging flowers. Consider creative writing or drama.
You spend much of your time caring for others.	a chance to be selfish. Allow yourself some time, space, money and energy and do just what you want. Don't feel that you have to apologize or explain.	making something for yourself; learn something you've always wanted to learn; engaging in nature study – birdwatching, collecting plant specimens.
Your life seems dull and unchallenging.	adventure. You needn't risk your neck. If the truly daring outdoor pursuits seem more than you can taken on, play a game for stakes.	kayaking, mountain climbing, hang gliding, scuba diving. Go out with a metal detector and seek buried treasure – even lost coins on the beach.

Handout 24 *cont.*

If your work is:	You might benefit from:	You should consider:
You feel like a failure at your work or in your personal life.	doing something that will give a feeling of achievement. Doing anything at all superbly can provide it. Spend time searching for the right thing.	selecting some field of knowledge that always interested you and becoming an expert in it – learning to speak a foreign language fluently, mastering a craft.
Your work involves persuading or instructing others.	stopping pushing. The mental muscles you use in trying to manoeuvre others often get tired and need resting. Do the things that let you hang loose.	taking in some sporting events, going to the theatre, listening to music. Raising houseplants may be just the thing – they won't talk back to you.
You work under direct supervision.	feeling you have independence of choice and action, with no one – not even yourself – judging your performance. Maybe you need to boss others.	captaining a little league team or organizing a neighbourhood study or discussion group. Get the family together and go jogging, bicycling, camping.
You work under deadline pressure.	forgetting about clocks and tightly scheduled activities.	pitching horseshoes, target shooting, roller skating, out-of doors?

Handout 24   *cont.*

If your work is:	You might benefit from:	You should consider:
	Try hard to avoid falling back into your work pattern. Play for the fun of it.	Give yourself an open-ended amount of time to construct a model. Go for a walk.
Your job is repetitive, routine.	a mental challenge. Stretch your mind with difficult games in which you must employ strategy, whether they be physical or sedentary.	tennis, golf or chess? Take a course. Go out to read your way through the Greek Books. Memorize some Shakespeare. Learn to play a musical instrument.
You work with machines.	getting out and rediscovering that the world of nature is much bigger – and a lot more soothing – than the world of machines.	cross-country skiing, camping, birdwatching? Since there's nothing so unmachinelike as water, anything you can do in or near the water might prove rewarding.
You work as a member of a team.	spending more time alone. Don't whatever you do, join another team.	one-on-one games such as chess, cribbage, or those you can play on your television screen. Throw a frisbee, go bicycling, jogging, try archery or photography.

Handout 24 *cont.*

If your work is:	You might benefit from:	You should consider:
You work mostly alone.	more social contact. Sitting at home with your stereo or coin collection is hardly the recreation for you.	joining a hobby club to further an interest you already have or to start you off on something new? Team sports might provide what you need.
You feel you are not doing anything for anyone else.	doing some giving. Spend time with someone who will appreciate your caring. Volunteering time and energy may be the most re-creating recreation of all.	helping a disabled child, reading to a blind person, driving an elderly patient to the doctor, teaching English to an immigrant family.

VALUE OF VARIOUS EXERCISES

Handout 25

Energy range* (Approximate calories used per hour)	Activity	Benefits
72–84	Sitting Conversing	Of no conditioning value.
120–50	Strolling, 1 m.p.h. Walking, 2 m.p.h.	Not sufficiently strenuous to promote endurance unless your exercise capacity is very low.
150–240	Cleaning windows Mopping floors Vacuuming	Adequate for conditioning if carried out continuously for 20–30 minutes.
	Bowling	Too intermittent; not sufficiently taxing to promote endurance.
	Walking, 3 m.p.h. Cycling, 6 m.p.h.	Adequate dynamic exercise if your capacity is low.
	Golf, pulling cart	Useful for conditioning if you walk briskly, but if cart is heavy, isometrics may be involved.
300–60	Scrubbing floors	Adequate endurance exercise if carried out in at least 2 minute stints.

Handout 25 *cont.*

	Walking, 3.5 m.p.h. / Cycling, 8 m.p.h.	Usually good dynamic aerobic exercise.
	Table tennis / Badminton / Volleyball	Vigorous continuous play can have endurance benefits. Otherwise, only promotes skill.
	Golf, carrying clubs	Promotes endurance if you reach and maintain target heart rate. Aids strength and skill.
	Tennis, doubles	Not very beneficial unless there is continuous play for at least 2 minutes at a time. Aids skill.
	Many calisthenics	Will promote endurance if continuous, rhythmic and repetitive.
	Ballet exercises	Promotes agility, coordination and muscle strength. Those requiring isometric effort, such as push-ups and sit-ups, not good for cardiovascular fitness.
360–420	Walking, 4 m.p.h. / Cycling, 10 m.p.h. / Ice or roller skating	Dynamic, aerobic and beneficial. Skating should be done continuously.
420–80	Walking, 5 m.p.h. / Cycling, 11 m.p.h.	Dynamic, aerobic and beneficial.
	Tennis, singles	Can provide benefit if played for 30 minutes or more with an attempt to keep moving.
	Water skiing	Total isometrics. Very risky for persons with high risk of heart disease or deconditioned normals.

Handout 24   *cont.*

Calories	Activity	Description
480–600	Jogging, 5 m.p.h. Cycling, 12 m.p.h. Downhill skiing	Dynamic, aerobic, endurance-building exercise. Runs are usually too short to promote endurance significantly. Mostly benefits skill. Combined stress of altitude, cold and exercise may be too great for some heart patients.
	Paddleball	Not sufficiently continuous. Promotes skill.
600–60	Running, 5.5 m.p.h. Cycling, 13 m.p.h.	Excellent conditioner.
Above 600	Running, 6 or more m.p.h.	Excellent conditioner.
	Handball	Competitive environment in hot room is dangerous to anyone not in excellent physical condition. Can provide conditioning benefit if played 30 minutes or more with attempt to keep moving.
	Squash	
	Swimming†	Good conditioning exercise – if continuous strokes. Especially good for persons who can't tolerate weight-bearing exercise, such as those with joint diseases.

* In all activities, energy used will vary depending on skill, rest patterns, environmental temperature and body size.
† Wide calorie range depending on skill of swimmer, stroke, temperature of water, body composition, current and other factors.

Bibliography

Abramson, L.Y., Seligman, M.E.P. and Teasdale, J. (1978) 'Learned helplessness in humans: critique and reformulation', *Journal of Abnormal Psychology*, 87: 49–74.

Antonovsky, A. (1987) *Unraveling the Mystery of Health: How People Manage Stress and Stay Well*. San Francisco: Jossey-Bass.

Beehr, T.A. (1981) 'Work role stress and attitudes towards coworkers', *Group Organizational Studies*, 6: 201–10.

Beehr, T.A. (1985a) 'Organizational stress and employee effectiveness: a job characteristics approach', in T.A. Beehr and R.S. Bhagat (eds), *Human Stress and Cognition in Organizations*. New York: John Wiley and Sons.

Beehr, T.A. (1985b) 'The role of social support in coping with organizational stress', in T.A. Beehr and R.S. Bhagat (eds), *Human Stress and Cognition in Organizations*. New York: John Wiley and Sons.

Beehr, T.A. (1987) 'The themes of social-psychological stress in work organizations', in A.W. Riley and S.J. Zaccaro (eds), *Occupational Stress and Organizational Effectiveness*. New York: Praeger.

Beehr, T.A. and Newman, J.E. (1978) 'Job stress, employee health and organizational effectiveness: a facet analysis, model, and literature review', *Personnel Psychology*, 31: 665–99.

Benson, H. (1975) *The Relaxation Response*. New York: Morrow.

Bonoma, T.V. and Slevin, D.P. (1978) *Executive Survival Manual*. Boston: CBI.

Breif, A.P., Schuler, R.S. and VanSell, M. (1981) *Managing Stress*. Boston: Little, Brown.

Brett, J.M. (1980) 'The effect of job transfer on employees and their families', in C.L. Cooper and R. Payne (eds), *Current Concerns in Occupational Stress*. New York: John Wiley.

Brown, B.B. (1984) 'Stress coping through biofeedback', in A.S. Sethi and R.S. Schuler (eds), *Handbook of Organizational Stress Coping Strategies*. Cambridge, MA: Ballinger.

Bulman, R.J. and Wortman, C.B. (1977) 'Attribution of blame and coping in the "real world": severe accident victims react to their lot', *Journal of Personality and Social Psychology*, 35: 351–63.

Burke, R.J. (1988) 'Sources of managerial and professional stress in large organizations', in C.L. Cooper and R. Payne (eds), *Causes, Coping and Consequences of Stress at Work*. London: John Wiley.

Cannon, W. (1935) Stresses and strains of homeostasis, *American Journal of Medical Sciences*, 189: 1–14.

Carver, C.S., Scheier, M.F. and Weintraub, J.K. (1989) 'Assessing coping strategies: a theoretically based approach', *Journal of Personality and Social Psychology*, 56: 267–83.

Chadrow, M.E. (1984) 'Job satisfaction, occupational stress and video display terminal work: an interaction model of person–environment fit', *Dissertation Abstracts International*, 44(8-b): 2548.

Cobb, S. (1976) 'Social support as a moderator of life stress', *Psychosomatic Medicine*, 38: 300–14.

Cohen, S. (1980) 'After effects of stress on human performance and social behavior: a review of research and theory', *Psychological Bulletin*, 88: 82–108.

Cohen, S. and Wills, T.A. (1985) 'Stress, social support, and the buffering hypothesis', *Psychological Bulletin*, 98: 310–57.

Constable, J.F. and Russell, D.W. (1986) 'The effect of social support and the work environment upon burnout among nurses', *Journal of Human Stress*, 12: 20–6.

Cooper, C.L. and Davidson, M.J. (1982) *High Pressure: Working Lives of Women Managers*. London: Fontana.

Cooper, C.L. and Marshall, J. (1976) 'Occupational sources of stress: a review of the literature relating to coronary heart disease and mental ill health', *Journal of Occupational Psychology*, 49: 11–28.

Cooper, C.L. (1987) 'The experience and management of stress: job and organizational determinants', in A.W. Riley and S.J. Zaccaro (eds), *Occupational Stress and Organizational Effectiveness*. New York: Praeger.

Cooper, K.H. (1982) *The Aerobics Program for Total Well-being*. New York: M. Evans.

Cox, T. (1980) 'Repetitive work', in C.L. Cooper and R. Payne (eds), *Current Concerns in Occupational Stress*. New York: John Wiley.

Cox, T. (1985) 'Repetitive work: occupational health and stress', in C.L. Cooper and M.J. Smith (eds), *Job Stress and Blue Collar Work*. New York: John Wiley.

Dainoff, M.J., Hurrell, J. and Happ, A. (1981) 'A taxonomic framework for the description and evaluation of paced work', in G. Salvendy and M.J. Smith (eds), *Machine Pacing and Occupational Stress*. London: Taylor and Francis.

Davis, R.V. and Lofquist, L.H. (1984) *A Psychological Theory of Work Adjustment: An Individual Differences Model and its Application*. Minneapolis: University of Minnesota Press.

Dynerman, S.B. and Hayes, L.O. (1991) *The Best Jobs in America for Parents Who Want Careers and Time For Children Too*. New York: Rawson Associates.

Ellis, A. (1978) 'What people can do for themselves to cope with stress', in C.L. Cooper and R. Payne (eds), *Stress at Work*. New York: John Wiley.

Evans, P. and Bartolome, F. (1986) 'The dynamics of work–family relationships in managerial lives', *International Review of Applied Psychology*, 68: 320–33.

Ferrini, P. and Parker, L.A. (1978) *Career Change*. Cambridge, MA: Technical Education Research Centres.

Fielding, J.E. and Breslow, L. (1983) 'Health promotion programs sponsored by California employer', *American Journal of Public Health*, 73: 538–42.

Fisher, R. and Ury, W. (1981) *Getting to Yes: Negotiating Agreement Without Giving In*. Boston, MA: Houghton Mifflin.

Ford, D.L. (1985) 'Job-related stress of the minority professional: an exploratory analysis and suggestions for future research', in T.A. Beehr and R.S. Bhagat (eds), *Human Stress and Cognition in Organizations*. New York: John Wiley.

Frankenhaeuser, M. and Gardell, B. (1976) 'Underload and overload in working life: outline of a multidisciplinary approach', *Journal of Human Stress*, 2: 35–45.

Frankenhaeuser, M. and Johansson, G. (1986) 'Stress at work: psychobiological and psychosocial aspects', *International Review of Applied Psychology*, 35: 287–99.

Frankenhaeuser, M., Lundberg, U. and Chesney, M. (eds) (1991) *Women, Work, and Health*. New York: Plenum.

French, J.R. (1973) 'Person role fit', *Occupational Mental Health*, 3: 15–20.

French, J.R. and Caplan, R.D. (1973) 'Organizational stress and individual strain', in A.J. Marrow (ed.), *The Failure of Success*. New York: AMACOM.

Friedman, M. and Ulmer, D. (1984) *Treating Type A Behavior and Your Heart*. New York: Knopf.

Friedman, M., Thoresen, C.E., Gill, J.J., Ulmer, D., Powell, L.H., Price, V.A., Brown, B., Thompson, L., Rabin, D.D., Breall, W.S., Bourg, E., Levy, R. and Dixon, T. (1986) 'Alteration of Type A behavior and its effect on cardiac recurrences in post-myocardial infarction patients: summary results of the recurrent coronary prevention project', *American Heart Journal*, 112: 653–65.

Gandz, J. and Murray, V.V. (1980) 'The experiences of work place politics', *Academy of Management Journal*, 23: 237–51.

George-Perry, S. (1988) 'Easing the costs of mental health benefits', *Personnel Administrator*, 33: 62–7.

Gibson, J.L., Ivancevich, J.M. and Donnelly, J.H. (1979) *Organizations: Behaviour, Structure, Processes*. Dallas: Business Publications.

Gibson, J.L., Ivancevich, J.M. and Donnelly, J.H. (1985) *Organizations*. Plano, TX: Business Publications.

Gray-Toft, P. (1980) 'Effectiveness of a counseling support program for hospice nurses', *Journal of Counseling Psychology*, 27: 346–54.

Greenhalgh, L. and Rosenblatt, Z. (1984) 'Job insecurity: toward conceptual clarity', *Academy of Management Review*, 9: 438–48.

Hall, D.T. (1976) *Careers in Organizations*. Pacific Palisades: Good Year.

Hall, D.T. (1986) *Career Development in Organizations*. San Francisco, CA: Jossey-Bass.

Harris, D.V. (1973) *Involvement in Sport: A Somatopsychic Rationale for Physical Activity*. Philadelphia, PA: Lea and Febiger.

Haskell, W.L. (1984) 'Overview: health benefits of exercises', in J.D. Matarazzo et al. (eds), *Behavioral Health*. New York: John Wiley.

Hayghe, H. (1986) 'Rise in mothers' labor force activity', *Monthly Labor Review*, 109: 43–5.

Hersey, J.C., Klibanoff, L.S., Lam, D.J. and Taylor, R.L. (1984) 'Promoting social support: the impact of California's "Friends Can Be Good Medicine" campaign', *Health Education Quarterly*, 11: 293–311.

Hiroto, D.S. (1974) 'Learned helplessness and locus of control', *Journal of Experimental Psychology*, 102: 187–93.

Holmes, T.H. and Masuda, M. (1974) 'Life change and illness susceptibility', in B.S. Dohrenwend and B.P. Dohrenwend (eds), *Stressful Life Events: Their Nature and Effect*. New York: John Wiley.

Holmes, T.H. and Rahe, R.H. (1967) 'The Social Readjustment Rating Scale', *Psychosomatic Medicine*, 11: 213–18.

House, J.S. (1981) *Work, Stress and Social Support*. London: John Wiley.

Howard, J.H. (1984) 'Stress and the manager: perspectives', in A.S. Sethi and R.S. Schuler (eds), *Handbook of Organizational Stress Coping Strategies*. Cambridge, MA: Ballinger.

Hunt, H.A. and Hunt, T.L. (1983) *Human Resource Implications of Robotics*. Kalamazoo, Upjohn Institute.

Hurrell, J.J. and Colligan, M.J. (1985) 'Alternative work schedules: flextime and the compressed work week', in C.L. Cooper and M.J. Smith (eds), *Job Stress and Blue Collar Work*. New York: John Wiley.

Ivancevich, J.M. and Donnelly, J.H. (1975) 'Relation of organizational structure to job satisfaction, anxiety-stress and performance: measures, research and contingencies', *Administrative Science Quarterly*, 20: 272–80.

Ivancevich, J.M. and Lyon, H.L. (1972) *Organizational Climate, Job Satisfaction, Role Clarity and Selected Emotional Reaction Variables in a Hospital Milieu*. Lexington, KY: Office of Business Development and Government Services.

Ivancevich, J.M. and Matteson, M.T. (1980) *Stress and Work: A Managerial Perspective*. Glenview, IL: Scott Foresman.

Ivancevich, J.M. and Matteson, M.T. (1988) 'Promoting the individual's health and well-being', in C.L. Cooper and R. Payne (eds), *Causes, Coping and Consequences of Stress at Work*. London: John Wiley.

Ivancevich, J.M., Matteson, M.T. and Preston, C. (1982) 'Type A behavior and physical well being', *Academy of Management Journal*, 25: 373–91.

Jackson, S.E. (1983) 'Participation in decision making as a strategy for reducing job-related strain', *Journal of Applied Psychology*, 68: 3–19.

Jackson, S.E. (1984) 'Organizational practices for preventing burnout', in A.S. Sethi and R.S. Schuler (eds), *Handbook of Organizational Stress Coping Strategies*. Cambridge, MA: Ballinger.

Jackson, S.E. and Maslach, C. (1982) 'After effects of job-related stress: families as victims', *Journal of Occupational Behavior*, 2: 63–77.

Jacobson, E. (1938) *Progressive Relaxation*. Chicago, IL: University of Chicago Press.

Jaremko, M.E. (1983) 'Stress inoculation training for social anxiety', in D. Meichenbaum and M.E. Jaremko (eds), *Stress Reduction and Prevention*. New York: Plenum Press.

Jette, M. (1984) 'Stress coping through physical activity', in A.S. Sethi and R.S. Schuler (eds), *Handbook of Organizational Stress Coping Strategies*. Cambridge, MA: Ballinger.

Jick, T.D. (1985) 'As the ax falls: budget cuts and the experience of stress in organizations', in T.A. Beehr and R.S. Bhagat (eds), *Human Stress and Cognition in Organizations*. New York: John Wiley.

Jokl, M.W. (1984) 'The psychological effects on man of air movement and the colour of his surroundings', *Applied Ergonomics*, 15: 119–26.

Kahn, R.L., Wolfe, D.M., Quinn, R.P., Snoek, J.D. and Rosenthal, R.A. (1964) *Organizational Stress: Studies in Role Conflict and Ambiguity*. New York: John Wiley.

Katz, R. (1985) 'Organizational stress and early socialization experiences', in T.A. Beehr and R.S. Bhagat (eds), *Human Stress and Cognition in Organizations*. New York: John Wiley.

Katz, D. and Kahn, R.L. (1978) *The Social Psychology of Organizations*. New York: John Wiley.

Kaye, B.L. (1982) *Up is Not the Only Way*. Englewood Cliffs, NJ: Prentice-Hall.

Kelly, M. and Cooper, C.L. (1981) 'Stress among blue collar workers', *Employee Relations*, 3: 6–9.

Kendall, P.C. and Bemis, K.M. (1983) 'Thought and action in psychotherapy: the cognitive-behavioral approaches', in M. Hersen, A.E. Kazdin and A.S. Bellack (eds), *The Clinical Psychology Handbook*. New York: Pergamon Press.

Ketz de Vries, M.F.R. (1984) 'Organizational stress management audit', in A.S. Sethi and R.S. Schuler (eds), *Handbook of Organizational Stress Coping Strategies*. Cambridge, MA: Ballinger.

Kopleman, R.E. (1986) *Managing Productivity in Organizations*. New York: McGraw-Hill.

Korman, A.K., Wittig-Berman, U. and Lang, D. (1981) 'Career success and personal failure: alienation in professionals and managers', *Academy of Management Journal*, 14: 342–60.

Kosecoff, J. and Fink, A. (1982) *Evaluation Basics: A Practitioner's Manual*. Newbury Park, CA: Sage.

Kramer, M. (1974) *Reality Shock: Why Nurses Leave Nursing*. St Louis: Mosby.

Kuna, D.J. (1975) 'Meditation and work', *Vocational Guidance Quarterly*, 23: 342–6.

Lawler, E.E., III (1986) *High-Involvement Management: Participative Strategies for Improving Organizational Effectiveness*. San Francisco, CA: Jossey-Bass.

Lazarus, A.A. (1976) *Multimodal Therapy*. New York: Springer.

Lazarus, R.S. and Folkman, S. (1984) *Stress, Appraisal, and Coping*. New York: Springer.

Lazarus, R.S. and Launier, R. (1978) 'Stress-related transactions between person and environment', in L.A. Pervin and M. Lewis (eds), *Internal and External Determinants of Behavior*. New York: Plenum.

Ledwidge, B. (1980) 'Run for your mind: aerobic exercise as a means of alleviating anxiety and depression', *Canadian Journal of Behavioral Science*, 12: 126–40.

Leiter, M.P. and Maslach, C. (1986) 'Role structure and burnout in the field of human services', *Journal of Applied Behavioral Sciences*, 22: 47–52.

Locke, E.A. and Latham, G.P. (1984) *Goal Setting: A Motivational Technique That Works*. Englewood Cliffs, NJ: Prentice-Hall.

London, M. (1985) *Development Managers: A Guide to Motivating and Preparing People for Successful Managerial Careers*. San Francisco, CA: Jossey-Bass.

London, M. and Mone, E.M. (1987) *Career Management and Survival in the Work Place*. San Francisco, CA: Jossey-Bass.

McGoldrick, A.F. and Cooper, C.L. (1985) 'Stress at the decline of one's career: the act of retirement', in T.A. Beehr and R.S. Bhagat (eds), *Human Stress and Cognition in Organizations*. New York: John Wiley.

McGrath, J.E. (1976) 'Stress and behaviour in organizations', in M. Dunnette (ed.), *Handbook of Industrial and Organizational Psychology*. Chicago: Rand McNally.

McLeod, A.G.S. (1985) 'EAP's and blue collar stress', in C.L. Cooper and M.J. Smith (eds), *Job Stress and Blue Collar Work*. New York: John Wiley.

Martin, J.E. and Dubbert, P.M. (1982) 'Exercise applications and promotion in behavioral medicine: current status and future directions', *Journal of Consulting and Clinical Psychology*, 50: 1004–17.

Maslach, C. and Jackson, S.E. (1981) 'The measurement of experienced burnout', *Journal of Occupational Behavior*, 2: 99–113.

Mason, J.L. (1980) *Guide to Stress Reduction*. Culver City, CA: Peace Press.

Mathney, K.B., Aycock, D.W., Pugh, J.L., Curlette, W.L. and Cannella, K.A. (1986) 'Stress coping: a qualitative and quantitative synthesis with implications for treatment', *The Counseling Psychologist*, 14: 499–549.

Matteson, M.T. and Ivancevich, J.M. (1987) *Controlling Work Stress: Effective Resource and Management Strategies*. San Francisco, CA: Jossey-Bass.

Meichenbaum, D. (1977) *Cognitive Behavior Modification: An Integrated Approach.* New York: Plenum.

Meichenbaum, D. (1985) *Stress Inoculation Training.* Elmsford, NY: Pergamon Press.

Mobley, W.H. (1982) *Employee Turnover: Causes, Consequences and Control.* Reading, MA: Addison-Wesley.

Monk, T.H. and Tepas, D.I. (1985) 'Shift work', in C.L. Cooper and M.J. Smith (eds), *Job Stress and Blue Collar Work.* New York: John Wiley.

Moos, R.H., Insel, P.M. and Humphrey, B. (1974) *Work Environment Scale.* Palo Alto, CA: Consulting Psychology Press.

Muchinsky, P.M. and Tuttle, M.L. (1979) 'Employee turnover: an empirical and methodological assessment', *Journal of Vocational Behaviour,* 14: 43–77.

Murphy, L.R. (1984) 'Occupational stress management: a review and appraisal', *Journal of Occupational Psychology,* 57: 367–72.

Murphy, L.R. (1985) 'Individual coping strategies', in C.L. Cooper and M.J. Smith (eds), *Job Stress and Blue Collar Work.* New York: John Wiley.

Murphy, L.R. and Hurrell, J.J. (1987) 'Stress management in the process of organizational stress reduction', *Journal of Managerial Psychology,* 2: 18–23.

Nahrwold, S.C. (1987) 'Employee assistance programs: managing organizational stress and strain', in A.W. Riley and S.J. Zaccaro (eds), *Occupational Stress and Organizational Effectiveness.* New York: Praeger.

Neale, M.S., Singer, J.A., Schwartz, J.L. and Schwartz, G.E. (1983) *YALE-NIOSH occupational stress project.* Paper presented to the 4th annual meeting of the Society of Behavioral Medicine, Baltimore, MD.

Nicholson, N. (1984) 'A theory of work role transitions', *Administrative Science Quarterly,* 29: 172–91.

Novaco, R.W. (1977) 'A stress inoculation approach of anger management in the training of law enforcement officers', *American Journal of Community Psychology,* 5: 327–46.

Osipow, S.H. and Davis, A.S. (1988) 'The relationship of coping resources to occupational stress and strain', *Journal of Vocational Behaviour,* 32: 1–15.

Osipow, S.H. and Spokane, A.R. (1987) *Manual for the Occupational Stress Inventory.* Odessa, FL: Psychological Assessment Resources, Inc.

Ostberg, O. and Nilsson, C. (1985) 'Emerging technology and stress', in C.L. Cooper and M.J. Smith (eds), *Job Stress and Blue Collar Work.* New York: John Wiley.

Otway, H.J. and Misenta, R. (1980) 'The determinants of operator preparedness for emergency situations in nuclear power plants', Paper presented at Workshop on Procedural and Organizational Measures for Accident Management: Nuclear Power Plants. International Institute for Applied Systems Analysis. Laxenberg, Austria, 28–31 January.

Parkerson, G.R., Broadhead, W.E. and Tse, C.K. (1990) 'The Duke Health Profile', *Medical Care,* 28: 1056–72.

Patton, M.Q. (1990) *Qualitative Evaluation and Research Methods.* Newbury Park, CA: Sage.

Payne, R. (1980) 'Organizational stress and support', in C.L. Cooper and R. Payne (eds), *Current Concerns in Occupational Stress.* New York: John Wiley.

Pearlin, L. and Schooler, C. (1978) 'The structure of coping', *Journal of Health and Social Behavior,* 19: 2–21.

Peter, L.F. and Hull, R. (1969) *The Peter Principle.* New York: William Merrow.

Pierce, J.L. and Newstrom, J.W. (1983) 'The design of flexible work schedules and employee responses: relationships and processes', *Journal of Occupational Behavior*, 4: 247–62.

Pines, A.M. and Aronson, E. (1981) *Burnout: From Tedium to Personal Growth*. New York: Free Press.

Poulton, E.C. (1978) 'Blue collar stressors', in C.L. Cooper and R. Payne (eds), *Stress at Work*. New York: Wiley.

Powell, L.H. (1984) 'Can the Type A Behavior Pattern be altered after myocardial infarction? A second year report from the Recurrent Coronary Prevention Project', *Psychosomatic Medicine*, 46: 293–14.

Preston, H.B. and Bierman, M.E. (1985) 'An insurance company's EAP produces results', *EAP Digest*, 5: 21–8.

Roskies, E. (1987) *Stress Management for the Healthy Type A: Theory and Practice*. New York: Guilford Press.

Russell, D.W., Altmaier, E.M. and VanVelzen, D. (1987) 'Job-related stress, social support, and burnout among classroom teachers', *Journal of Applied Psychology*, 72: 269–74.

Rutenfranz, J., Haider, M. and Koller, M. (1985) 'Occupational health measures for night workers and shift workers', in S. Folkard and T.H. Monk (eds), *Hours of Work: Temporal Factors in Work Scheduling*. Chichester: John Wiley.

Salvendy, G. (1981) 'Classification and characteristics of paced work', in G. Salvendy and M.J. Smith (eds), *Machine Pacing and Occupational Stress*. London: Taylor and Francis.

Sauter, S.L., Murphy, L.R. and Hurrell, J.J. (1990) 'Prevention of work-related disorders', *American Psychologist*, 45: 1146–58.

Schneider, B. and Schmitt, N. (1986) *Staffing Organizations*. Pacific Palisades, CA: Scott, Foresman.

Schuler, R.S. (1977) 'Role conflict and ambiguity as a function of the task–structure–technology interaction', *Organizational Behavior and Human Performance*, 20: 60–74.

Schuler, R.S. (1980) 'Definition and conceptualization of stress in organizations', *Organizational Behavior and Human Performance*, 24: 115–30.

Schuler, R.S. (1984) 'Organizational stress and coping: a model and overview', in A.S. Sethi and R.S. Schuler (eds), *Handbook of Organizational Stress Coping Strategies*. Cambridge, MA: Ballinger.

Schuler, R.S. and Sethi, A.S. (1984) 'Time management and leader communication behavior', in A.S. Sethi and R.S. Schuler (eds), *Handbook of Organizational Stress Coping Strategies*. Cambridge, MA: Ballinger.

Seligman, M.E.P. (1975) *Helplessness: On Depression Development, and Death*. San Francisco, CA: Freeman.

Selye, H. (1956) *The Stress of Life*. New York: McGraw-Hill.

Sethi, A.S. (1984a) 'Meditation for coping with organizational stress', in A.S. Sethi and R.S. Schuler (eds), *Handbook of Organizational Stress Coping Strategies*. Cambridge, MA: Ballinger.

Sethi, A.S. (1984b) 'Yoga for coping with organizational stress', in A.S. Sethi and R.S. Schuler (eds), *Handbook of Organizational Stress Coping Strategies*. Cambridge, MA: Ballinger.

Shadish, W.R., Cook, T.D. and Leviton, L.C. (1991) *Foundations of Program Evaluation: Theories of Practice*. Newbury Park, CA: Sage.

Smith, M.J. (1985) 'Machine-paced work and stress', in C.L. Cooper and M.J. Smith (eds), *Job Stress and Blue Collar Work*. New York: John Wiley.

Smith, R.E. (1979) *The Subtle Revolution*. Washington, DC: The Urban Institute.

Smith, T.W. and Pope, M.K. (1990) 'Cynical hostility as a health risk: current status and future directions', *Journal of Social Behavior and Personality*, 5: 77–88.

Sorensen, G. and Verbrugge, L.M. (1987) 'Women, work, and health', *American Review of Public Health*, 8: 235–51.

Steward, N. (1978) *The Effective Woman Manager*. New York: John Wiley.

Stoney, C.M., Langer, A.W., Sutterer, J.R. and Gelling, P.D. (1987) 'A comparison of biofeedback-assisted cardiodeceleration in Type A and B men: modification of stress-associated cardiopulmonary and hemodynamic adjustments', *Psychosomatic Medicine*, 109: 79–87.

Stufflebeam, D.L. and Shinkfield, A.J. (1985) *Systematic Evaluation*. Boston/The Hague/Dordrecht/Lancaster: Kluwer-Nijhoff.

Suedfeld, P. (1979) 'Stressful levels of environmental stimulation', in I.G. Sarason and C.D. Speilberger (eds), *Stress and Anxiety* (Vol. 6). *The Series of Clinical and Community Psychology*. Washington, DC: Hemisphere.

Suinn, R.M. (1982) 'Interventions with Type A Behaviors', *Journal of Consulting and Clinical Psychology*, 6: 933–49.

Sutherland, V.J. and Cooper, C.L. (1990) *Understanding Stress: A Psychological Perspective for Health Professionals*. London: Chapman and Hall.

Taylor, F.W. (1911) *Principles of Scientific Management*. New York: Harper and Row.

Terborg, J.R. (1985) 'Working women and stress', in T.A. Beehr and R.S. Bhagat (eds), *Human Stress and Cognition in Organizations*. New York: John Wiley.

Turner, A.N. and Lawerence, R.P. (1965) *Industrial Jobs and the Worker*. Cambridge, MA: Harvard University Graduate School of Business Administration.

Wall, I.D. and Clegg, C.W. (1981) 'A longitudinal study of group work redesign', *Journal of Occupational Behavior*, 2: 31–49.

Wallace, M., Levens, M. and Singer, G. (1988) 'Blue collar stress', in C.L. Cooper and R. Payne (eds), *Causes, Coping and Consequences of Stress at Work*. New York: John Wiley.

Walsh, D. (1982) 'Employee assistance programs', *Milbank Memorial Fund Quarterly/Health and Society*, 60(3).

Wanous, J. (1969) *Organizational Entry*. Reading, MS: Addison-Wesley.

Wanous, J. (1980) *Organizational Entry*. Reading, MS: Addison-Wesley.

Weiss, R. (1974) 'The provisions of social relationships', in Z. Rubin (ed.), *Doing Unto Others*. Englewood Cliffs, NJ: Prentice-Hall.

Wells, J.A. (1984) 'The role of social support groups in stress coping in organizational settings', in A.S. Sethi and R.S. Schuler (eds), *Handbook of Organizational Stress Coping Strategies*. Cambridge, MA: Ballinger.

Williams, D.R. and House, J.S. (1985) 'Social support and stress reduction', in C.L. Cooper and M.J. Smith (eds), *Job Stress and Blue Collar Work*. New York: John Wiley.

Wolf, S. and Wolff, H.G. (1943) *Gastric Function: An Experimental Study of a Man and His Stomach*. New York: Oxford University Press.

Wolshok, M.L. (1981) *Blue Collar Women: Pioneers on the Male Frontier*. New York: Anchor.

Woodward, J. (1965) *Industrial Organizations: Theory and Practice*. London: Oxford University Press.

Worthen, B. and Sanders, J. (1987) *Educational Evaluation: Alternative Approaches and Practical Guidelines*. New York: Longman.

Wortman, C., Biernat, M. and Lang, E. (1991) 'Coping with role overload', in M. Frankenhaeuser, U. Lundberg and M. Chesney (eds), *Women, Work, and Health*. New York: Plenum Press.

Index